★ KITCHEN MOJO ★

KITCHEN MOJO

*120+ easy recipes
to sink your teeth into*

PAUL MERCURIO

MURDOCH BOOKS

Contents

Finding your
KITCHEN MOJO

Too often I meet people who tell me they never cook, can't cook, they're too busy to cook, they find cooking scary or boring ... or they admit that they're just too plain lazy to cook. Frankly, I can't understand it—I mean, I have to cook, it's in my blood. If I haven't cooked something for a day or two I go stir crazy (even just typing these words I start to think about cooking up a stir-fry!). I'm obsessed with preparing lovely plates of all sorts of delicious things. I love cooking, I need to cook and if I am not cooking, well, I tend to lose my mojo for everything.

Food is life. Without eating we will wilt until we no longer exist and, when you think about it, life is about energy, creativity, love, laughter, nourishment, family, friends, happiness, harmony, fulfilment ... to name just a few of the reasons we live. As we get on with living our lives we spend a lot of our most meaningful moments breaking bread—with family, friends, colleagues and even strangers. So when someone says to me they don't like cooking, what I'm hearing is that they've lost their mojo for living! You see, being connected to your mojo is about having a zest for life (now I'm thinking of lemon curd cake). Cooking is a celebration of all the good things about life and that's why finding your kitchen mojo is so important. It's about nourishing yourself on all sorts of levels and then nourishing those around you. No recipe is too simple, too easy, too complicated or too hard—they are just wonderful opportunities to get your mojo on, express your creativity, entertain your friends, feed the family or treat yourself.

Contrary to popular belief, no one is born a master chef—it takes years of experience and many failures along the way to attain that mantle. That said, we don't need to be a master chef to cook a cracking good meal, we just need to understand a few basics, such as if you cook something over high heat you will probably burn it! In fact, the very best bit of advice I've ever heard about cooking on a barbecue was 'For heaven's sake, just turn it down!' I was certainly guilty of thinking cooking on a barbecue meant turn it up high, chuck the meat on, turn it lots and take it off once it was blackened! Therein lies our first important piece of advice on cooking well—temperature control.

This book is not aimed at teaching you how to cook, there are plenty of books and websites that do that. Instead, my aim is to help you find your kitchen mojo so you can embrace your inner chef—yes, we all have one—to take that leap of faith into the kitchen and give it a go. Hopefully, along the way you will discover that you do actually like cooking, you are actually good at it and above all it is fun!

Cheers and happy cooking!

CHAPTER 1

Home
ALONE

*I*t's an unfortunate fact that when most people find themselves at home on their own at dinner time they can't be bothered to make something nice to eat. It's as if our thought patterns are saying, 'I'm on my own, so I don't deserve a nice meal. I'll just have a piece of toast with some melted cheese and a glass of water!' Well, let me suggest to you that just because you're on your own doesn't mean you don't deserve a terrific and nutritious meal.

These days, cooking a meal for one has never been easier; you no longer have to buy a bunch of celery when you only need one stick; heck, you can even buy peeled and measured-out cut up ingredients all ready to throw in a pot and make a soup or homemade curry; and you can buy just the right amount of salad ingredients to make a fantastic dish without incurring the wrath of the leftover gods or finding said leftovers several weeks later in the back of the fridge well past their use-by date.

But why go to the effort of cooking just one meal when there are plenty of frozen and premade, unfrozen, prepackaged or ready-to-go cooked meals out there, I hear you ask. Well, there's nothing wrong with an occasional prepackaged feed when you feel like slacking off in front of the TV. Mind you, anything you buy prepackaged was probably cooked a few days or weeks ago, so there will be a compromise on flavour. Nor is there anything wrong with going down to your local Thai place for a freshly cooked takeaway if you don't feel up to facing the kitchen yourself. But when you do make the effort to cook for one you'll be giving yourself total control of what you eat—not only will you be giving yourself flavour and freshness, you'll also have absolute control of the amount of salt, saturated fat, preservatives, carbs and sugars in the meal, and be able to ensure that each meal has the right balance of food groups.

The most important point for me, though, in cooking for one is taking it as an opportunity to cater just for myself. I love it when I'm home alone for meals because I can cook whatever I feel like at the time without having to think about what other people want. It also means I can cook all the things I love to eat that my wife, kids and friends don't. See what I mean? Cooking a special meal for one can actually be pretty exciting. It doesn't have to be an effort. In fact, it can be a joy—not only are you nourishing your body with good food, you are nourishing your soul by doing something for yourself that makes you feel good, feel happy and feel worthy.

When I was making movies in Los Angeles I would get on set at five in the morning and head straight to the catering truck and order a burrito. They were fantastic (which I am sure had a lot to do with the fact that Mexican chefs were at the helm who knew how to cook burritos to perfection). The chefs used a chorizo paste and blended that into the eggs, making them spicy and creamy and adding a lovely bit of heat that helped me wake up. My breakfast burritos aren't quite as good as the ones from that catering truck, but they are still pretty delicious for breakfast … or lunch or dinner!

BREAKFAST BURRITO

1 tablespoon unsalted butter
2 short-cut bacon rashers, diced
80 g (2¾ oz) chorizo sausage, diced
2 free-range eggs
2 tablespoons milk
pinch of ground chipotle chillies (optional)*
1 large firm tomato, quartered, skin and seeds
   removed, finely diced
½ red onion, very finely diced

1 tablespoon coriander (cilantro) leaves, chopped
1 tablespoon sliced pickled jalapeño chillies
1 lime
salt
1 large corn tortilla
1 tablespoon sour cream
25 g (1 oz/¼ cup) grated good quality cheddar
   cheese

Melt the butter in a frying pan over high heat. Add the bacon and chorizo and fry for 4–5 minutes so they develop good colour and get a little crispy.

Crack the eggs into a bowl, add the milk and ground chipotle, if using, then beat together. Don't worry about seasoning as there is plenty of seasoning in the bacon and chorizo.

Reduce the heat to medium, add the egg mixture to the pan and use a spatula to gently fold the eggs and meat together. Continue doing this for 3–4 minutes or until the eggs are just set—remember the residual heat will continue to cook the eggs after you remove them from the heat. Remove the pan from the heat and set aside while you make the salsa.

Combine the tomato, onion, coriander and jalapeño in roughly equal amounts. Add a squeeze of lime to taste and a pinch of salt, then mix and taste for balance and adjust accordingly.

To assemble, put the tortilla on a plate and zap it in the microwave for about 20 seconds to warm it up. Spread the sour cream over the tortilla. Sprinkle about 1½ tablespoons of the tomato salsa over the tortilla, then lay the cooked egg mixture down the centre of the tortilla. Sprinkle the grated cheese over the egg.

Next, roll up the tortilla. Starting with the bottom, fold it up and over the eggs so the first 2 cm (¾ in) is covered, then repeat with the top part of the tortilla, folding it down 2 cm (¾ in) from the top. Fold the right side of the tortilla over the eggs to completely cover them, then fold over the left side as tightly as possible without tearing the tortilla. The top and bottom ends should be tucked in so nothing can fall out. It is now a burrito! Cut the burrito in half and eat!

Feeds 1

NOTE

Chipotle chillies are dried smoked jalapeño chillies. They are hot, smoky, earthy and add great flavour and aroma to all sorts of dishes.

An omelette seems to me to be one of the most perfect home alone feasts. They are easy to cook and you can flavour them with whatever takes your fancy and whatever you have in the fridge.

EASY OMELETTE

2 free-range eggs
2 tablespoons milk
salt and freshly ground black pepper
¼ teaspoon chilli powder (optional)
2 teaspoons butter
5 slices smoked chicken breast
3 slices red onion
3 slices tomato
30 g (1 oz/⅓ cup) grated cheddar cheese
small handful of baby spinach leaves

A couple of my other favourite filling combinations

3 slices smoked salmon (just enough to cover the
    bottom half of the omelette)
4 steamed asparagus spears
3 slices avocado
2 slices red onion
3 slices tomato
3–4 slices emmental cheese
1–2 teaspoons tzatziki

3 slices roast pork
2 spring onions (scallions), sliced

1–2 tablespoons tinned red kidney beans
1 tablespoon hot salsa
15 g (½ oz/⅓ cup) shredded lettuce
3–4 slices smoked cheese
1 tablespoon sliced pickled jalapeño chillies

3–4 pieces marinated goat's cheese, crumbled
50 g (1¾ oz/¼ cup) cooked pumpkin cubes
    (fried or steamed)
3 slices red onion
1 tablespoon sultanas (golden raisins)
1 tablespoon toasted pine nuts
handful of rocket (arugula)

60 g (2¼ oz/⅓ cup) shredded barbecued chicken
2 spring onions (scallions), sliced
2 tablespoons tinned corn kernels
1–2 tablespoons barbecue sauce
3 long thin slices raw zucchini (courgette)
3 slices tomato
4 slices cheese (such as cheddar, smoky cheddar,
    emmental)

»→

◄─◄◄

Preheat the oven grill to high or 230°C (450°F) (fan-forced 210°C/415°F).

Crack the eggs into a bowl, add the milk and beat to combine. Season with salt and pepper, and the chilli powder if you like that little chilli kick.

Heat a 22 cm (8½ in) non-stick ovenproof frying pan over medium–high heat and then add the butter. When the butter has melted and covers the entire bottom of the pan, tip in your beaten egg mixture and gently swirl to evenly cover. Use a soft spatula and poke it around the sides of the pan, pulling the cooking egg away from the side and tilting the pan to allow any raw or runny egg mixture to fill any gaps. Continue to cook gently for about 5 minutes. You want the bottom of the omelette to cook but not burn, so you will probably need to turn the heat down once the egg has set.

When most of the egg has set but the top of the omelette is still a little runny, take the pan off the heat and pop it under the hot grill for 3 minutes to set the top—it will puff up and become fluffy. Carefully remove the pan from the grill and return to the stovetop over low heat. Put the smoked chicken, onion and tomato on top of one half of the omelette, leaving the other half bare. Place the pan back under the grill for a minute to warm the tomatoes through. Next, add the cheese to the other side of the omelette. Put the pan under the grill again and heat until the cheese has melted. Return the pan to the stove over medium–high heat and add the spinach to the pan, on top of the tomato, and warm through.

Now comes the tricky part—folding the omelette! Use your soft spatula and poke down the side of the pan to make sure the omelette is not stuck anywhere, then carefully slide the spatula under the top half with the melted cheese to make sure it is not stuck underneath. Gently shake the pan in a circular motion so the omelette is able to slide. Poke the spatula under the top half of the omelette (the cheese half) and flip it up and over the bottom half (the spinach and chicken half) so that it closes like a book. Don't worry if the two halves don't match up evenly—it will still taste great and practice will make you perfect in no time. Now, carefully using your spatula as a guide, slide the omelette out of the pan and onto a plate.

Eat!

Feeds 1

NOTE: You can add other flavours to your beaten egg in addition to chilli powder—smoky paprika, ground cumin and fresh chopped herbs like parsley, dill or coriander (cilantro).

>>>>>>>>>>>>>>>>>>>>>>>>>>>
TIP
As you can see, you really can use whatever combination gets you excited—even slices of lobster with a tartare sauce, rocket and avocado with chopped coriander (cilantro) leaves mixed through the eggs or, if you really want to push the envelope, how about tinned smoked oysters with pickled vegetables and a tablespoon of hot Thai sweet and sour sauce?
>>>>>>>>>>>>>>>>>>>>>>>>>>>

Caesar salad is one of my favourites and on those odd occasions when I find myself at home alone it is one of my 'go to' dishes. All you should need to buy to get started are four or five cos lettuce leaves from the fruit and veg store. The other ingredients you should already have stored away in your pantry or the fridge, and if you don't, then here's a hint: put them on your shopping list as must-buys for your kitchen next time you go to the store.

CAESAR SALAD

4–5 cos (romaine) lettuce leaves
2 teaspoons butter
1 bacon rasher, rind removed, roughly chopped
1 thick slice sourdough bread, cut into small cubes
2 teaspoons olive oil

2 tablespoons whole-egg mayonnaise
¼ teaspoon dijon mustard
1 teaspoon lemon juice
1 teaspoon olive oil
1 tablespoon freshly grated parmesan cheese
freshly ground black pepper

Dressing
½ garlic clove, crushed (more like ¼ clove as you don't use the garlic left in the crusher)
1 anchovy fillet, chopped

Preheat the oven to 180°C (350°F) (fan-forced 160°C/315°F).

You can either leave the lettuce leaves whole or tear them in half. Put the lettuce leaves in a salad bowl. Heat the butter in a frying pan over high heat, add the bacon and fry until it starts to get a little crispy, then remove and add to the lettuce bowl.

Put the bread cubes in a separate bowl, pour over the olive oil and toss to combine. Transfer to a baking tray, pop it in the oven and toast until golden and crisp. Remove from the oven and add the croutons to the salad bowl.

Put the garlic, anchovy, mayo, mustard, lemon juice, oil and parmesan in a small bowl and whisk until well combined. Season with pepper and pour over the salad. Toss well so all of the lettuce is evenly coated.

As well as being a great meal in itself, caesar salad goes well with anything barbecued, crumbed or beer-battered! So, if you are home alone tonight, cook up a crumbed pork chop, make this salad and then sit back with a beer or a cool glass of wine and enjoy the peace and quiet.

Feeds 1

NOTE

For a more traditional Caesar you could add a soft-boiled egg to ooze some lovely yolky flavour. To do this, put a free-range egg in a small saucepan with cold water over high heat and bring to the boil. As soon as it starts to boil set a timer to 3 minutes and then remove the egg at the 3-minute mark. Put the egg under cold running water and when cool enough to handle carefully peel it. Once peeled it should be all soft and squishy which means the yolk is still nice and runny! You could add some warmed-through slices of smoked chicken to make it a chicken Caesar salad.

I ummed and ahhed about putting this salad in this chapter because it is a great salad, simple to make, delicious and filling ... and therefore a great recipe for the family, a barbecue gathering or for eating with mates while watching the footy. That said, it is quick and easy to prepare, no mess, no fuss, and therefore the perfect salad for when you are home alone. It is filling enough to be a meal in itself or you could have it with something barbecued, roasted, pan-fried or baked.

CHORIZO AND BEAN SALAD

2 teaspoons olive oil
50 g (1¾ oz) chorizo, roughly chopped
150 g (5½ oz/¾ cup) tinned four-bean mix, drained
6 slices red onion
4 cherry tomatoes, quartered
60 g (2¼ oz/⅓ cup) diced cucumber
10 g (¼ oz) rocket (arugula), torn
2 tablespoons chopped flat-leaf (Italian) parsley

Dressing
2 teaspoons olive oil
2 teaspoons red wine vinegar
¼ garlic clove, crushed
salt and freshly ground black pepper

Heat the olive oil in a small frying pan over medium–high heat. When hot add the diced chorizo. Cook for about 4 minutes, stirring until it is nicely coloured and crispy. Remove the pan from the heat.

Put all the remaining salad ingredients in a salad bowl and toss to combine. Add the chorizo and mix through.

To make the dressing, put all the ingredients in a small screw-top jar and shake to combine. Pour the dressing over the salad and toss again.

I told you it was simple, easy, no fuss and no mess! Since you are home alone you can eat it straight out of the salad bowl so you have next to no washing up.

Feeds 1

Salad for one? Yes, yes, yes! It is pretty easy to scale this up for four people, but it is a delicious salad when you are on your own. As for any leftover veggies at the end of assembling this salad, use them in my kitchen sink frittata on page 222.

COUSCOUS AND ROAST VEGGIE SALAD

½ small red onion

1 garlic clove, unpeeled

¼ small Japanese or Lebanese eggplant (aubergine)

¼ small zucchini (courgette)

¼ small carrot

2 teaspoons olive oil

80 ml (2½ fl oz/⅓ cup) chicken stock (preferably homemade)

pinch of salt

½ teaspoon butter

65 g (2⅓ oz/⅓ cup) couscous

1 tablespoon pine nuts, toasted in a dry frying pan

4 yellow teardrop tomatoes or cherry tomatoes, quartered

35 g (1¼ oz) sultanas (golden raisins)

1 tablespoon chopped flat-leaf (Italian) parsley

Dressing

1 teaspoon orange juice

1 teaspoon lemon juice

1 teaspoon olive oil

salt and freshly ground black pepper

Preheat the oven to 180°C (350°F) (fan-forced 160°C/315°F).

Put the onion, garlic, eggplant, zucchini and carrot in a bowl, drizzle with the olive oil and toss to evenly coat. Spread the vegetables on a baking tray and cook for 20–30 minutes until tender. Remove the vegetables from the oven and, when cool enough to handle, roughly chop. Discard the skin from the garlic and chop that also, then put everything into a salad bowl and mix to combine.

Bring the stock to the boil in a saucepan over high heat. Add the salt and butter and stir until melted through. Put the couscous in a bowl and pour over the stock mixture. Stir, then cover and leave for about 10 minutes or until the couscous is cooked. Use a fork to fluff up and separate the grains.

Put the cooked couscous, toasted pine nuts, tomatoes, sultanas and parsley in the bowl with the roast veggies and mix well to evenly combine.

Put the orange juice, lemon juice and olive oil into a small screw-top glass jar and shake to combine. Season with salt and pepper to taste and then shake again. Pour the dressing over the salad and give it all a final mix, then serve.

Feeds 1

TIP

This is a great salad on its own but it would also go perfectly as a side with beer and herb–marinated chicken on page 142, oven-roasted tandoori lamb leg on page 151, barbecued lamb ribs on page 71, pulled pork on page 72, grilled gin-marinated quail on page 67 ... yes, I'm thinking it goes well with pretty much everything in this book!

You can make this dish as easy as you want by buying a marinara mix from your fishmonger, or you can get all fancy and make your own mix by buying a couple of prawns, a few scallops, a couple of rings of calamari and maybe even a Moreton Bay bug tail. The important thing here is great quality, super-fresh seafood, so I would always advocate sourcing your seafood from your local fishmonger.

SPAGHETTI MARINARA

125 g (4½ oz) linguine
1 tablespoon olive oil
1 anchovy fillet
1 garlic clove, finely chopped
½ red bird's-eye chilli, finely chopped (optional)
150 g (5½ oz) good quality marinara mix (or your own combination)*

1 large tomato, roughly diced
60 ml (2 fl oz/¼ cup) good quality dry white wine (I would recommend a chardonnay)
4 basil leaves
salt and freshly ground black pepper

Cook the linguine in a large saucepan with plenty of boiling salted water, following the packet instructions, until *al dente*.

Meanwhile, heat the olive oil in a non-stick frying pan over medium–high heat. Add the anchovy, garlic and chilli, if using, and cook for about 4 minutes or so. You will need to stir this and use the back of your spoon to break the anchovy down so that it melts away and becomes part of the oil. Also be careful not to burn the garlic. Add the marinara mix and stir through so the mix is well coated with the oil, and continue to cook and stir for the next 3 minutes or until the prawns start to become opaque. You do not want to cook the seafood all the way through at this point or else it will become overcooked when you cook the sauce. Add the chopped tomato and wine, bring to a simmer, then simmer for about 5 minutes or so until the seafood is cooked through and the wine has reduced. Add the basil leaves, season with salt and pepper, and remove from the heat.

When the pasta is cooked, use tongs to pick the linguine out of the water and transfer directly into the frying pan with the sauce. Give it all a good mix and then serve in a bowl.

Feeds 1

NOTE

If you use prawns in your marinara, select raw prawns. Going to a good fishmonger for seafood is the best option, as you know the quality, freshness and flavour will be topnotch. You can also buy frozen prawns and seafood at large supermarkets for convenience—just take out what you want and keep the rest frozen. Make sure, though, that you thaw your seafood out either on a plate, covered, in the fridge, or leave them on a plate, covered, on your work surface until just thawed. Keep an eye on the cat though. Once thawed, cook immediately.

This is one of my all-time favourite pastas! It became known as 'whore's pasta' or Puttanesca because prostitutes in Naples needing a good feed to keep their energy up would cook it between clients. It's really easy to prepare and takes as long to make as it does for the water to boil, and the pasta to cook. Traditionally, it was made with black olives, but I love this dish with Spanish stuffed green olives.

SPAGHETTI PUTTANESCA

125 g (4½ oz) spaghetti
1 tablespoon olive oil
3 anchovy fillets, chopped
1 small garlic clove, finely chopped
1 red bird's-eye chilli, finely chopped including the seeds for heat
45 g (1⅔ oz/¼ cup) Spanish stuffed green olives, roughly chopped

1 tablespoon capers (if using large capers chop them, if using the tiny ones don't)
1 large or 2 medium ripe tomatoes, roughly chopped
10 basil leaves, roughly torn
freshly ground black pepper
1–2 tablespoons freshly grated parmesan cheese

Cook the spaghetti in a large saucepan with plenty of boiling salted water, following the packet instructions, until *al dente*.

Meanwhile, heat the olive oil in a large frying pan over medium–high heat, then add the anchovies. They will spit a bit and smell quite strong when they cook, but fear not, the flavour they add to the dish is not fishy! Use the back of a wooden spoon to mash the anchovy into the oil and cook for 2–3 minutes. If they spit too much, turn the heat down a little. Next, add the garlic and the chilli, and cook for another couple of minutes, being careful not to burn the garlic. Add the olives and capers, and cook for a couple of minutes to heat through, then add the tomato and half the basil and a turn or two from the pepper grinder. Reduce the heat to medium and cook gently until the pasta is ready. You really don't need to cook the sauce much—it is more about heating the ingredients so all the flavours combine and allowing the tomatoes to wilt a little.

Once the pasta is cooked, add the rest of the basil to the puttanesca, then use tongs to pick the pasta from the water and transfer into the frying pan with the sauce. It is good to get a little bit of the pasta water into the sauce, which is why I use the tongs. Give it all a good stir and, if you think it is a little dry, just add a little more of the cooking water and stir again.

Serve in a bowl and top with parmesan.

Feeds 1

》》》》》》》》》》》》》》》》》》》》》》》》
TIP
Some people suggest adding olive oil to the pan when cooking pasta to stop it sticking together, but I reckon it stops the sauce from sticking to the pasta! So to prevent pasta sticking together, just stir it occasionally while it is cooking.
》》》》》》》》》》》》》》》》》》》》》》》》

This is one of those recipes that I have been cooking for years, in fact, it was the first risotto I ever cooked and has taught me the art of making risotto. To me, it also encapsulates what Italian cooking is all about, and that is using only a few ingredients to create a simple yet wonderfully flavoured dish. If you have never used dried porcini mushrooms before you are in for a treat, however, they do have a big flavour so less is more until you get the hang of them.

RED WINE, PORCINI AND ITALIAN SAUSAGE RISOTTO

500 ml (17 fl oz/2 cups) chicken stock (preferably homemade)

2 g (1/10 oz) dried porcini mushrooms (they are very strong flavoured so this should be plenty)

2–3 Italian sausages (about 125 g/4½ oz in total), such as pork and fennel or pork and chilli—quality is key!

55 ml (1¾ fl oz) olive oil

1 teaspoon butter

½ small onion, finely diced

110 g (3¾ oz/½ cup) arborio rice

60 ml (2 fl oz/¼ cup) dry red wine (a shiraz or cabernet–merlot would work well)

75 g (2⅔ oz/½ cup) frozen peas

salt and freshly ground black pepper

25 g (1 oz/¼ cup) freshly grated parmesan cheese

Put the chicken stock in a saucepan and bring to a very gentle simmer.

Place the dried porcini mushrooms in a bowl and cover with boiling water. Leave to soak until you need them or for at least 30 minutes.

Use a sharp knife to slit the sausage skin from top to bottom and peel the skin away from the meat. Put the meat in a bowl and break it up with a wooden spoon. Heat 1 tablespoon of the olive oil in a saucepan over medium–high heat. Add the broken-down sausage meat and cook, stirring frequently and using the back of a wooden spoon to break it up so you don't get any large clumps—it should look like minced meat. Because you are going to add this to your risotto later you don't need to cook the meat completely through at this stage, so once browned remove it from the saucepan and set aside in a bowl.

Using the same saucepan (you want to use the flavour from cooking the sausages), reduce the heat slightly to medium and add the butter and remaining olive oil. When the pan is hot add the onion. Cook gently, stirring occasionally, until the onion is soft and starts to smell sweet—say about 5 minutes. Add the arborio rice and mix thoroughly to coat. Cook and stir for several more minutes to toast the rice a little—it won't change colour, but it will build flavour.

These days, cooking a meal for one has never been easier ... I love it when I'm home alone because I can cook whatever I feel like without having to think about what other people want.

Take the mushrooms out of the soaking liquid and squeeze out the excess water. Reserve the liquid. Chop the mushrooms finely, then add to the pan along with about 1 tablespoon of the soaking liquid. Stir through well. When all the liquid has been soaked up by the rice, add the red wine and stir well. This is where heat management comes into play—you don't want the heat too high as it will make the rice absorb the liquid too quickly, and you don't want it too low as it will not absorb properly. Once the wine has been absorbed by the rice, add 60 ml (2 fl oz/¼ cup) of chicken stock and stir through. For the next 30 minutes continue to stir the rice and add about 60 ml of stock every 5 minutes or so.

After you add the stock for the sixth time, also stir in the peas. You can add them frozen if you want, or whack them in the microwave for 30 seconds first. When you add stock for the seventh time, add your partially-cooked sausage, stirring well to combine and finish the meat cooking. Taste the rice to see if it is done—if it is still a little crunchy in the middle, add a final 60 ml of stock and stir through until it is absorbed. Season the risotto and stir through the parmesan. Serve in a bowl with a glass of red, if there is any left—well you have to do something while you do all that stirring, right?

I know you will enjoy!

Feeds 1

I read somewhere that 'Arrabbiata' literally means 'angry', and thus this pasta sauce gets it name from the 'anger' or 'heat' in its chilli kick. How much heat you want to include is up to you. If you don't want any heat, then don't put any chilli in and use a mild pancetta—you will still have a very full-flavoured sauce. The rule I work with is big-flavoured sauces use big pasta shapes, so rigatoni is perfect for this dish.

PORK ARRABBIATA RIGATONI

2 tablespoons olive oil

¼ small Japanese eggplant (aubergine), cut into 5 mm (¼ in) cubes

¼ small zucchini (courgette), cut into 5 mm (¼ in) cubes

2 anchovy fillets, chopped

1 small garlic clove, sliced

½ red bird's-eye chilli, finely chopped

25 g (1 oz) hot pancetta, chopped into lardons*

½ red capsicum (pepper), thinly sliced

8 kalamata olives, pips removed, torn apart

1 tablespoons tomato paste (concentrated purée)

2 pork and fennel sausages (about 125 g/4½ oz each), skin removed

½ tin (200 g/7 oz) chopped tomatoes

60 ml (2 fl oz/¼ cup) dry red wine

8 basil leaves

salt and freshly ground black pepper

125 g (4½ oz) rigatoni

25 g (1 oz/¼ cup) freshly grated parmesan cheese

Heat 1 tablespoon of the olive oil in a frying pan over medium–high heat. Add the eggplant and zucchini, and fry, turning frequently, until browned, then transfer them into a bowl and set aside.

Put the remaining oil in the pan and reheat. Add the chopped anchovies and cook for several minutes, stirring often. Add the garlic and chilli and cook for a couple of minutes, continuing to stir so the garlic doesn't burn. Next, add the pancetta and capsicum and fry for a further 3 minutes or until the meat starts to caramelise and the capsicum has softened. Add the olives and cook for 2 minutes, then add the tomato paste and cook out for 2 minutes, stirring constantly. Turn the heat up to high, add the sausage mince and break it down using the back of a wooden spoon. Continue to stir so that the meat browns evenly. Add the tomatoes, wine, a tablespoon or two of water and half the basil leaves, mix everything together well and bring to the boil. Reduce the heat and simmer gently for about 15 minutes, stirring occasionally. Taste for seasoning, add the remaining basil leaves and the reserved eggplant and zucchini and simmer for another 15 minutes or so giving it a stir every now and then.

Meanwhile, cook the rigatoni in a large saucepan with plenty of boiling salted water, following the packet instructions, until *al dente,* then drain. Add the cooked pasta to the frying pan, if it's big enough, and mix well. If the frying pan is too small, return the pasta to the saucepan, tip in the sauce and mix well.

Serve in a bowl sprinkled with the parmesan.

Feeds I

NOTE

'Lardons' is the French term for small matchstick-cut pieces of bacon.

This is an elegantly simple way to cook fish. All the flavours in the parcel beautifully combine and create, not just a wonderful dish, but a wonderful sauce as well. You could also cook this directly on the coals of a fire if you happen to be camping in the great outdoors.

ITALIAN FISH PARCELS

25 g (1 oz) butter

3 thin slices lemon

5 pieces marinated red capsicum (pepper), thinly sliced

1 small piece marinated roasted eggplant (aubergine), thinly sliced

1 teaspoon chopped dill

1 firm white-fleshed fish fillet (about 200 g/7 oz), such as snapper, barramundi or blue-eye cod

3 very thin slices red onion

4 sun-dried tomatoes, diced

¼ teaspoon capers

6 kalamata olives, pips removed, torn apart

4 basil leaves, torn

½ teaspoon chopped flat-leaf (Italian) parsley

1 tablespoon olive oil

freshly ground black pepper

Preheat the oven to 200°C (400°F) (fan-forced 180°C/350°F).

Lay out a sheet of foil big enough to wrap the fish and then lay another piece on top. Smear or rub some of the butter onto the foil, then place the lemon slices, capsicum and eggplant in the centre. Add the dill and then put the fish fillet on top. Arrange the onion slices over the fish and scatter over the tomato, capers, olives, basil and parsley. Drizzle the olive oil over everything, put small dobs of the remaining butter on top and season with pepper. Wrap the double foil around the fish, bringing each side up and twisting together to create a neat, tightly sealed parcel. The fish will steam as well as roast in the parcel.

Put the parcel on a baking tray in the oven and cook for about 10–15 minutes, depending on the thickness of the fish. Carefully open the foil and check the fish— it is cooked if it easily flakes apart when prodded with a fork. Serve the parcel on a plate, then unwrap and eat directly out of the parcel, savouring all the lovely cooking juices.

Feeds 1

So a lot of people said to me making pizza dough for one would be too much work and no one would want to do it BUT it is not too much work and it TASTES HEAPS BETTER than those store-bought pizzas. Also, while you leave the dough to rise you could walk the dog, vacuum the lounge room, relax and read the paper or just prep your toppings! And then, if you're going to the trouble of making your own base, making your own sauce is pretty easy too (although, okay, a store-bought tomato base or a couple of tablespoons from a jar of pasta sauce will also work). Seriously though, homemade pizza does taste great and you know it's completely fresh and doesn't have any hidden additives, and it's bound to be better for you too. So why not give it go?

PIZZA

One-Ball Pizza Dough
1 teaspoon dried yeast
⅛ teaspoon olive oil
⅛ teaspoon sugar
110 g (3¾ oz/¾ cup) plain (all-purpose) flour
   or strong flour*
⅛ teaspoon salt

Sauce (optional)
1 tablespoon olive oil
½ small onion, finely chopped
1 small garlic clove, crushed
¼ teaspoon dried basil
¼ teaspoon dried oregano or marjoram
2 teaspoons tomato paste (concentrated purée)
1 tablespoon dry red wine (optional, but delicious)
1 large ripe tomato, finely diced
salt and freshly ground black pepper
pinch of sugar

Suggested Toppings
bocconcini and fresh basil leaves
roast pumpkin, goat's cheese, pine nuts and
   rocket (arugula)
spicy salami, kalamata olives, roast capsicum
   (pepper), marinated artichokes and anchovies
cooked pork and fennel sausage slices, red kidney
   beans, sliced red onion, avocado and sliced
   pickled jalapeño chillies
good-quality deli-bought ham slices, marinated
   capsicum (pepper) and crushed pineapple
barbecued chicken, sliced spring onions (scallions),
   sun-dried tomatoes, fresh spinach and sliced
   pickles

50–100 g (1¾–3½ oz/½–1 cup) pizza cheese mix

Put 80 ml (2½ fl oz/⅓ cup) of warm water in a clean small bowl or glass jug (pitcher), then add the yeast, olive oil and sugar. Give it a stir and then set aside to let the yeast activate. After about 10–15 minutes you should have some foam or froth on the top of the yeast solution.

   Put the flour and salt in a mixing bowl and combine. You can do this in an electric mixer or by hand. Once the yeast mix has become thick and a little frothy add it to the flour and combine using an electric mixer fitted with a dough hook or a wooden spoon until it forms a ball. Tip the dough onto a lightly floured work surface and knead—it should be slightly sticky, which is good. If it is too sticky, sprinkle a little more flour over the dough and knead some more. Continue to knead until it becomes quite soft and smooth, then form it into a smooth ball.

Get a small bowl and spray or wipe the inside with oil and then sprinkle a little flour around the inside of the bowl so that it sticks to the oil—this will stop the dough from sticking to the bowl while it rises. Put the dough in the bowl and cover with plastic wrap. Set aside for an hour or so in a warm place (in winter it may take 2 hours) until it doubles in size.

Preheat the oven as hot as it will go!

If you are making your own pizza sauce, heat the olive oil in a frying pan over medium heat. Add the onion and cook for several minutes or until soft and translucent. Add the garlic and dried herbs and cook, stirring for another couple of minutes and then add the tomato paste and cook, continuing to stir, for another 2 minutes. Stir in the wine, if using, and then add the tomato, including any juices, and stir through. Finally, add the salt, pepper and sugar, stir to combine and then simmer very gently for 10 minutes. If the sauce gets too thick you can add a little water to loosen it although it should be a thick, rich sauce. Remove the sauce from the heat and use a stick blender or food processor to purée until smooth. Put the sauce in a bowl in the fridge until needed. Here is a good tip—never put hot sauce on to your pizza dough as it will heat the dough and make it stick to the work surface or the paddle, making it very difficult to get it in the oven!

What to top it with? As far as toppings go, the world is your oyster—and there are some suggestions to the left to get you going. Whatever you use, don't forget the cheese at the end! I buy a pizza cheese mix from the supermarket which has three grated cheeses—cheddar, parmesan and mozzarella—that I keep in the freezer in between pizza-making bouts.

Prepare a pizza pan, baking tray or a pizza stone by brushing it with a little olive oil.

Once you have organised your topping and the dough has risen, roll the dough out into a circle the size of your pizza pan. Place your dough on the pizza pan then use a pastry to brush some oil over the top of your rolled out dough. Place the pan on the middle rack of your oven and pre-cook the dough until slightly browned. When you lift up one side of the dough it shouldn't sag in half but stay fairly straight. I pre-cook my base because most domestic ovens can't get hot enough to cook the base through when it has all the toppings on. If you cook on a pizza stone then you probably won't have to pre-cook your dough. Remove from the oven, spread evenly with sauce and then add your topping. Sprinkle cheese over the top to cover and then return to the oven and cook until the cheese has melted and started to colour a little. Remove from the oven and eat!

Feeds I

NOTE

Double '0' flour, 00 flour, Doppio Flour or even bread flour are all known as strong flour— used for making breads. Since pizza dough is a type of bread, then using this sort of flour will give better results. That said, normal plain flour will work as well.

This curry is so easy and simple to make that I am always amazed at how good it tastes. Of course, the secret is in using great quality ingredients and super-fresh fish. You could make your own curry paste, but nowadays there are some really terrific ones being sold in gourmet grocery stores, farmers' markets and supermarkets so you don't need to if you don't want to.

MASSAMAN FISH CURRY

1 tablespoon peanut oil
¼ red onion, thinly sliced
½ red capsicum (pepper), thinly sliced
1 tin (165 ml/5⅓ fl oz) coconut milk
2 tablespoons massaman curry paste*
juice of ½ lime (about 2 teaspoons)
2–3 drops fish sauce

1 white-fleshed fish fillet (about 150 g/5½ oz), such as snapper, flake, ling or flathead
5 snow peas (mangetout), top and tailed, halved
5 sugarsnap peas, top and tailed
¼ small zucchini (courgette), cut into batons
1 tablespoon coriander (cilantro) leaves

Heat the peanut oil in a non-stick frying pan over medium heat. Add the sliced onion and fry gently for about 3 minutes, stirring often. Add the capsicum and fry for a further 5 minutes. (You don't want to burn the onions, but I quite like bringing them to the point where they start to go a little brown for added flavour.) Add the coconut milk and curry paste, stirring well to combine, and bring to a simmer. Next, add the lime juice and fish sauce, stirring to combine, then taste for flavour. Put the fish fillet in the centre of the pan, scatter the vegetables around the sides, turn the heat down and simmer the sauce gently, covered with a lid. Turn the fish after 5 minutes and stir the vegetables so they are well coated with the sauce. Put the lid back on and cook for another 5 minutes. Turn again and check for doneness. The fish should easily flake apart once it is cooked—the total cooking time should be between 10 to 15 minutes, depending on the thickness of the fish fillet. Finish with the coriander, and serve with rice.

Feeds I

NOTE

Store-bought curry pastes are really convenient and really tasty, however, I would urge you to read the listed ingredients before buying. If the first ingredient is oil then don't buy it; the first ingredient should be a flavour like onion, chilli or lemongrass. Also, some of these pastes use palm oil which I don't like for health and ethical reasons. Ultimately, though, the decision is yours.

Stir-fry—the perfect one-pot, one-serve way of cooking. Well, that is if you can actually keep it to a one-person serve! It seems that no matter how hard I try, I still cook enough for two! Below will feed one person and you shouldn't have any leftovers, except some odds and ends you could save for an omelette or my kitchen sink frittata on page 222. I reckon once you've cooked this dish it will become a regular when you're home alone, but it's also pretty easy to upscale so you can share it with family and friends.

SESAME SICHUAN CHICKEN

4 dried shiitake mushrooms

1 tablespoon sichuan pepper (or dry-roasted sichuan peppercorns, ground using a mortar and pestle)

1 teaspoons sherry

2 teaspoons sesame oil

4 chicken tenderloins (about 200 g/7 oz in total), sliced

1 tablespoon olive oil or peanut oil

½ small red onion, halved then cut into five pieces

½ garlic clove, finely chopped

½ red bird's-eye chilli, finely chopped

½ cheek red capsicum (pepper), thinly sliced

5 snow peas (mangetout), top and tailed

5 sugarsnap peas, top and tailed

1 bok choy (pak choy) stem, roughly chopped

1 teaspoon soy sauce

1 teaspoon oyster sauce

30 g (1 oz) glass noodles, soaked in boiling water until soft, cut up using kitchen scissors before you drain them

Put the shiitake mushrooms in a small bowl, cover with boiling water and leave to soak for 30 minutes. Put the sichuan pepper, sherry and sesame oil in a separate bowl and stir well to combine. Add the sliced chicken and stir to coat. Cover with plastic wrap and set aside.

Put your wok on the stovetop over high heat, add half the olive oil and when it begins to smoke carefully tip in the chicken. As soon as the meat hits the pan stir vigorously for about 1–2 minutes, making sure the meat gets turned over and evenly sears. Tip back into the marinating bowl.

Next, add the remaining oil to the pan and when hot, but not smoking, add the onion and cook for a couple of minutes, breaking the pieces down with a wooden spoon. Add the garlic, chilli and capsicum and let it cook for another 2 minutes, stirring occasionally. Meanwhile, remove the shiitake mushrooms from the soaking water, squeeze out the excess moisture and cut in half. Add the mushrooms, snow peas, sugarsnaps and bok choy, and give it a really good stir to combine. Continue to cook for a couple of minutes, then add the soy sauce and oyster sauce and give it another good stir. Turn the heat down to medium, put the lid on and let the veggies steam for several minutes. Finally, return the chicken to the pan to finish the cooking process, then add the drained cut noodles and stir. Put the lid back on and cook for a few minutes more to heat through. Serve in a bowl and eat!

Feeds 1

> **TIP**
> The important thing to remember when cooking a stir-fry is that once you start it all happens pretty quickly, so chopping and preparing all the ingredients and having them in bowls ready to be tipped into the wok is the best habit to get into.

I was thinking about calling this dish 'Full of Flavour Beef Stew' because that is what it is, but then I hesitated because I thought this might make it sound like a lot of effort for a dish for one and people wouldn't bother. Well, this dish is 'full of flavour', but it's not complicated at all—it's a true one-pot wonder. You would be mad to go out and buy a pizza or some other takeaway when you could treat yourself to this hearty, nourishing and deliciously simple stew.

SIMPLE BEEF STEW

35 g (1¼ oz/¼ cup) plain (all-purpose) flour
½ teaspoon paprika
salt and freshly ground black pepper
200 g (7 oz) chuck steak, cut into 2.5 cm (1 in) cubes
2 tablespoons olive oil
½ brown onion, chopped
2 garlic cloves, chopped
1 small carrot, diced

1 celery stalk, diced
½ tin (200 g/7 oz) chopped tomatoes
250 ml (9 fl oz/1 cup) beef stock
1 tablespoon worcestershire sauce
10 green beans
2 tablespoons flat-leaf (Italian) parsley (optional)

Preheat the oven to 180°C (350°F) (fan-forced 160°C/315°F).

Put the flour in a bowl and mix in the paprika, salt and about ¼ teaspoon of black pepper. Add the beef and toss to coat.

Heat 1 tablespoon of the olive oil in a flameproof casserole dish over medium–high heat. Shake the excess flour from the beef, add to the dish and cook, stirring regularly until the meat is browned on all sides. Transfer the meat into a bowl and cover loosely with foil to keep warm.

Heat the remaining oil in the dish, add the onion and fry for about 3–4 minutes until softened. Add the garlic, carrot and celery and cook for another 5 minutes. Add the tomatoes, browned beef and any resting juices from the bowl, and stir through. Bring to the boil, then add the beef stock and worcestershire sauce. Bring back to the boil and season with salt and pepper. Cover with the lid, transfer to the oven and cook for about 1 hour. Add the beans, return to the oven and cook for another 15 minutes or until the beans are tender. Garnish with parsley, if you like, and serve over steamed rice, cooked pasta shapes or mashed potatoes.

Feeds 1

NOTE

You could also include potato in this stew. Just cut 1 medium–large potato into six pieces and add it to the casserole dish after the stew has been in the oven for about 30 minutes.

Crumbs! I love to crumb! Coating your meat in breadcrumbs is a great way for it to retain moisture during the cooking process, and it's also a great way to add other seasoning flavours to your meal. Different sorts of crumbs will add different flavours and textures to your dish, and different crumbs go well with different meats. Panko crumbs are all the rage now and are great on a variety of things, but who can resist the classic combination of breadcrumbs with parmesan cheese and fresh parsley mixed through to make a crumb—wonderful! The process is very simple and the results are truly delicious.

CRUMBED PORK CHOP

30 g (1 oz/½ cup) panko crumbs or dry
  breadcrumbs
2 tablespoons freshly grated parmesan cheese
35 g (1¼ oz/¼ cup) plain (all-purpose) flour

salt and freshly ground black pepper
1 pork chop (about 250 g/9 oz), rind removed
1 free-range egg, beaten in a large bowl
olive oil, for shallow-frying

Put the crumbs and parmesan in a bowl and mix to combine. Tip the crumb mixture onto a large plate and spread out evenly.

Put the flour in a plastic bag and season with salt and pepper. Add the pork chop, twist the top of the bag and then give it a shake to coat the chop. Remove the chop from the bag and shake off the excess flour. Dip the chop in the beaten egg to completely cover, then use a fork to take it out and place it on top of the parmesan crumbs. Scoop the crumbs around the sides and over the top of the chop, press down, and then turn the chop over and repeat the process. Make sure to press the crumbs into the sides as well so that the chop is completely covered.

Pour some olive oil in a frying pan, about 1 cm (½ in) deep, then heat over medium–high heat until you can see it shimmering. You don't want it smoking as you will burn the crumbs straight away. A good way to test if the oil is ready is to stick one end of the chop in the oil—if it doesn't sizzle or is slow to sizzle, remove the tip of the chop and allow the oil to get a little hotter.

Once the oil is sizzling nicely, gently lay the chop in the pan. Cook your chop for about 3 minutes or so until it starts to colour a little, then turn it over and cook for the same amount of time. Reduce the heat a little and turn the chop over again. You want the crumbs to gradually go a lovely golden colour—if the chop starts to brown quickly, turn the heat down some more. Continue to cook for another 15 minutes, turning the chop regularly, until it is cooked through and evenly golden on the outside. If the oil is too cool then it will soak into the crumbs and make your chop oily, if it is too hot it will burn the crumbs before the meat is cooked, so getting the temperature right is important.

Place the beautiful golden, crispy chop on paper towel to drain any excess oil, then transfer onto a plate. Serve with a side salad or some steamed baby brussels sprouts and roast potato.

Feeds 1

>>>>>>>>>>>>>>>>>>>>>>>
TIP
What to do with any leftover crumbs and beaten egg? Don't throw them out, make a crumb cake! Put the leftover crumbs and any herbs you like into the egg mix and combine. Add the crumbs gradually to get a good consistency—too many crumbs and it will be too dry, not enough crumbs and it will be too wet. Shape into a patty about 1.5–2 cm (about ¾ in thick) and fry it alongside your pork chop, turning it when you turn your chop. I love these patties with a little mango and chilli chutney.
>>>>>>>>>>>>>>>>>>>>>>>

Roast for one—super easy, super delish and you get gravy too! A lamb rack is by far the easiest cut of meat to roast for one, not only because of its handy size, but because the rack will have some fat on it which will baste itself as it cooks, and should make it melt-in-your-mouth tender when done. As for the veggies to serve it with, well this is really up to you, but I've included some suggestions here and, after all, what roast would be complete without a baked potato?

ROAST RACK OF LAMB

1 small roasting potato, peeled and halved

1 small sweet potato, peeled and cut into the same size and quantity as the potato

1 small brown onion, peeled

3 garlic cloves, unpeeled

2 tablespoons olive oil

four-point lamb rack*

¼ teaspoon lemon pepper

2 rosemary sprigs

75 g (2⅔ oz/½ cup) frozen peas, steamed in the microwave for 2 minutes, to serve

Gravy

1 heaped teaspoon plain (all-purpose) flour

1 tablespoon wine (red or white)

salt and freshly ground black pepper

Preheat the oven to 180°C (350°F) (fan-forced 160°C/315°F).

Put the vegetables, including the onion and garlic, in a large bowl, drizzle with half the olive oil and toss to evenly coat. Rub the remaining oil over the lamb rack and then season with the lemon pepper and sprinkle over the rosemary sprigs. Place the lamb and vegetables in a roasting tin and cook for 50–60 minutes. If you prefer your lamb on the pinker side, check it after 30–40 minutes—when cooked to your liking, remove the lamb from the tin and set aside covered with foil to rest. Continue to cook your vegetables until they are done to perfection then remove from the oven and put on a plate. Turn the oven off and put the plate along with the lamb in the oven to keep warm while you make the gravy.

To make the gravy, put your roasting tin on the stovetop over a medium–high heat and add the flour to the juices in the tin. Use a fork or a wooden spoon to stir the flour, scraping up all the caramelised remains from the meat and veg. Add the wine (my wife tends to use white, I tend to use red and, even occasionally, beer), and stir through. (If you don't want to use alcohol, then just use water or some vegetable stock.) Add 60 ml (2 fl oz/¼ cup) of water and stir vigorously to cook out any lumps, then season with salt and pepper to taste. Check your plate in the oven for any juice from the lamb rack and add that to the gravy.

To serve, remove the plate from the oven, add the cooked peas and spoon over the gravy. Enjoy with a glass of whatever you used to make the gravy (unless you used stock ... that would be weird!).

Feeds 1

NOTE

A four-point rack refers to how many rib bones are sticking out—one rib being one point. So if you buy a four-point rack you will have four rib bones sticking up.

TIP

If you have ever wondered why your lamb rack is a little tough and overcooked, it's probably because you did in fact cook it to perfection in the oven, but it cooked to over-perfection once you took it out. It's better to undercook the lamb slightly and then let it finish cooking while it is resting.

There is only really one reason I get excited if my wife tells me she is going away and that is this recipe. You see, my wife is not a big fan of lamb shanks, whereas I love them in all their soft, gelatinous glory, and when she heads out the door I immediately think 'Shanks for dinner!' Don't get me wrong, I don't wish my wife would go away more often ... but this is definitely the upside.

BEER-BRAISED LAMB SHANKS

35 g (1¼ oz/¼ cup) plain (all-purpose) flour
¼ teaspoon ground cumin
¼ teaspoon chilli powder
salt and freshly ground black pepper
2 lamb shanks (about 300 g/10½ oz in total)
1 tablespoon olive oil
½ red onion, thinly sliced

2 cheeks red capsicum (pepper), thinly sliced
2 tablespoons chopped mint
125 ml (4 fl oz/½ cup) good quality porter or stout beer
125 ml (4 fl oz/¼ cup) veal or beef stock*
2 tablespoons flat-leaf (Italian) parsley

Preheat the oven to 180°C (350°F) (fan-forced 160°C/315°F).

Put the flour, cumin, chilli, salt and pepper in a plastic bag and shake to combine. Add the shanks to the bag and give it a good shake to coat the meat. Dust the excess flour from the shanks.

Heat the olive oil in a flameproof casserole dish over medium–high heat. Add the shanks and cook for 3–5 minutes, turning regularly to brown the meat on all sides. Remove the shanks and set aside. Put the onion, capsicum and mint in the dish and then place the shanks on top. Pour in the beer and stock and bring to the boil, then cover with the lid, transfer to the oven and cook for about 1½ hours or until the meat is tender and falling off the bone.

Remove the shanks from the casserole dish, put in a bowl and cover loosely with foil to keep warm. Check the remaining ingredients in the pan—they should have cooked down to a thick sauce consistency. If it is too runny, place the casserole dish back on the stovetop over a high heat to reduce. Serve the shanks on a bed of garlic potato mash (see page 42) with steamed snake (yard-long) beans or green beans. Spoon over the sauce, and garnish with parsley.

Feeds I

NOTE

You can also get some great powdered stock in tins these days, so it is easy to make any amount of stock you need.

Okay, so you are home alone, it's 6 pm and cold and dark outside, it's winter and it's raining, and you feel like something simple, warming and filling—a hug on a plate. You look in the fridge and you have a couple of snags (hopefully good quality pork and fennel or beef and tomato), you have some green beans and a potato. Perfect! Fry up your snags, steam your beans and make a lovely creamy mash. Here's how.

POTATO MASH

1 large potato, such as desiree, peeled, halved lengthways and then cut into three pieces
1–2 teaspoons butter

60 ml (2 fl oz/¼ cup) milk
salt and freshly ground black pepper

Put the potato in a saucepan, cover with plenty of cold water and add a generous pinch of salt. Bring to the boil over high heat and then reduce the heat to a firm simmer. (If you rapid boil for the whole cooking time the potato will get soggy.) You'll know the potato is ready if you insert a sharp knife or a fork all the way into it without any resistance. Tip the potato into a colander to drain and then return the potato to the pan over very low heat. Use a fork or a potato masher to mash the potato, then add the butter and some of the milk and mash some more— you may not need all the milk, so add a little at a time. Continue to mash until the potato is smooth and the consistency is nice and fluffy. Season with salt and pepper and stir through.

Feeds 1

NOTE: To make garlic mash add half a clove of crushed garlic when you add the milk and butter.

But don't stop at plain potato mash or garlic mash, there are other mashed veggie options you can try.

To make a pumpkin mash just use pumpkin or use equal amounts of pumpkin and potato to make a mixed mash. You could also add carrot if you want to really mix it up, however, the carrot will take quite a bit longer than the pumpkin or potato to cook, so cook that first for about 10 minutes then add the potatoes and pumpkin.

Celeriac is great in a mash, too, check out page 165 and quarter the amounts if cooking for one.

To make a herb mash, add finely chopped herbs of your choice at the same time as you season the mash and stir through well. Good herbs to use are chives, dill, parsley or tarragon—just make sure you match the herb to the flavour of the rest of the meal.

Some people would say 'A soufflé for one, are you crazy!' To which I would reply, 'A soufflé for one, because you deserve it.' Just because you are home alone for whatever reason doesn't mean you don't deserve to be spoilt and have something special, something sweet, something truly delicious and decadent. And guess what, it's actually pretty easy to make, so get going.

CHOCOLATE AND RASPBERRY SOUFFLÉ

1 teaspoon unsalted butter, plus extra to line the soufflé dish

1 tablespoon caster (superfine) sugar, plus extra to line the soufflé dish

1 free-range egg (use eggs from a 700 g/ 1 lb 9 oz carton)

1 teaspoon plain (all-purpose) flour

60 ml (2 fl oz/¼ cup) very warm milk

1 tablespoon cocoa powder

25 g (1 oz) chocolate (either 75% cocoa or dairy milk or coconut-infused), finely chopped

15 frozen raspberries, thawed to room temperature

1 tablespoon sifted icing (confectioners') sugar

Preheat the oven to 190°C (375°F) (fan-forced 170°C/325°F).

Rub some butter around a soufflé dish or ramekin and then sprinkle in some caster sugar. Turn the soufflé dish around so that the sugar sticks to the butter and coats the inside of the dish completely and evenly.

Separate the egg. Beat the egg yolk in a bowl and whisk the white in a mixing bowl until stiff peaks form (see note). Set both bowls aside.

Melt the butter in a small saucepan over medium heat. When it begins to foam gradually add the flour, a little at a time, whisking constantly. Once all the flour is added continue to whisk for another couple of minutes—this is called a roux. When you see the roux start to darken a little, gradually add the milk, whisking constantly—the roux will become quite thick at first, but you don't want it to be lumpy. You should now have a thick creamy yellow paste. Continue to whisk, gradually adding the cocoa powder, caster sugar and chocolate until well combined. Sometimes, during this whole process I will take the saucepan off the heat as I whisk and then put it back on, mainly to help with the whisking but also to temper the heat a little. The resultant mixture in your saucepan will be quite thick. »→

NOTE

A quick word on beating egg whites—firstly, you must use a very clean bowl to whisk your whites or they will not rise. Secondly, you must make sure you do not have any egg yolk in the whites or they will not rise. Thirdly, you must not have any egg shell in your whites because that is just plain unprofessional!

◄─◄◄

Take a spoonful of the chocolate mixture, let it cool slightly, then add to the beaten egg yolk and whisk well to combine. Add this mixture to the saucepan with the chocolate sauce and mix together well.

Next, take a spoonful of the egg white and mix into the chocolate sauce. You can be firm about this as you want the egg whites to loosen the sauce and be mixed in well. Now mix, or rather fold through, the rest of the egg white, but this time you need to be gentle as you want to keep as much air in the whites as possible. At this point add the raspberries. Once the egg white has been folded through, pour the mixture into your prepared soufflé dish and place it in the centre of your oven. Cook for about 20 minutes. If you must look at your soufflé rising do it through the glass and not by opening the oven door. Don't be tempted. Just let the soufflé do its thing!

Remove the soufflé from the oven, sprinkle the icing sugar over the top and then eat. You could serve a small bowl of vanilla ice cream on the side or pour over some cream.

Feeds 1

PS: If you really want to make this for two here are the quantities:

2 teaspoons unsalted butter
1 tablespoon caster (superfine) sugar, plus 1 teaspoon extra
1 free-range egg yolk, beaten
2 free-range egg whites, beaten until stiff peaks form
1 tablespoon plain (all-purpose) flour
80 ml (2½ fl oz/⅓ cup) milk, very warm
50 g (1¾ oz) chocolate (either 75% or dairy milk or coconut-infused), finely chopped
1 tablespoon cocoa powder
30 frozen raspberries, thawed to room temperature
2 tablespoons icing (confectioners') sugar

The hardest thing to make for one is most probably dessert. I mean, it is pretty easy to grab an apple, cut up an orange or perhaps indulge in some fresh berries and a scoop of vanilla ice cream. But, just in case you feel like treating yourself with something a little more fancy, here's an idea that's pretty easy to make and well worth the small amount of effort.

FRUIT TART

1 sheet puff pastry
2–3 teaspoons mixed nut paste
½ apple, core removed

½ peach, stone removed
1 teaspoon raw sugar
1 free-range egg, beaten

Preheat the oven to 200°C (400°F) (fan-forced 180°C/350°F).

Cut the pastry sheet into four equal squares—keep one and put the rest back in the freezer for another time. Remove the plastic backing from the pastry and discard, then lay the piece of pastry on a baking tray lined with baking paper. Using a sharp knife, but not cutting all the way through, mark a line about 1 cm (½ in) in from the edge of the pastry all the way around—you will have drawn a square or border. Brush this border with a little beaten egg—reserve the rest of the beaten egg for an omelette or give it to the dog for a treat.

The nut paste I use has nothing in it except almonds, cashews and brazil nuts—no added oil or flavours. Spoon and spread this over the pastry so it fills within the square that you marked out, but do not cross over the line. Next, thinly slice the apple and the peach and layer them over the nut mix, alternating between each layer (see tip). Sprinkle the sugar over the top and place in the middle of the oven. Cook for about 25–30 minutes until the pastry has risen around the border and the fruit has softened. Make sure the bottom of the tart pastry is cooked through especially in the middle where all the fruit is sitting.

Remove from the oven and place the tart on a plate. Serve with mint and honey yoghurt (see note), a dollop of ice cream or cream.

NOTE: Combine 3 tablespoons of Greek-style yoghurt, 1 teaspoon of finely chopped mint and 1–2 teaspoons of honey for a delicious accompaniment to fruit tarts or baked fruit desserts.

Other toppings I like are thin slices of mango and thin slices of beurre bosc pear—these are the brown-skinned pears you see at the fruit shop. You could also use sliced strawberries and honeydew melon; beautiful summer figs sliced and layered with some blue cheese; or blood plum, nectarine and kiwi fruit.

Feeds 1

>>>>>>>>>>>>>>>>>>>>>>>>>
TIP
Be generous with the amount of fruit you put on the pastry as it really shrinks down.
>>>>>>>>>>>>>>>>>>>>>>>>>

CHAPTER 2

Footy's ON

*W*hat's the ultimate food to serve up when you have a bunch of friends over to watch the footy, or the motorcycle grand prix or the latest instalment of *Game of Thrones*? Well, I guess it's up to you how much effort you're going to go to. You could buy some nuts and dips, and a few packets of chips. That's pretty easy, unmemorable and, some would say, lazy. Or you could impress your friends and their tastebuds by making something really delicious and truly unique. These recipes range in difficulty from super easy to pretty easy, to more time consuming—and that is the point. None of the recipes are difficult to make, some just take more time, and sometimes the more time you put in the more enjoyment you get out. Even better, get your friends, family or neighbours over and into the kitchen to help out. This food is supposed to be eaten with friends and it's also supposed to be made with friends. Ultimately, this chapter is about great party food: food that goes well with a beer, a cider or a glass of wine; food that is best enjoyed in company; food that is fun to make and, most importantly; food that makes you feel good.

Enjoy!

51

If you ask me I will tell you all the snacks in this chapter are great, and I make all of them all the time. This recipe is inspired by the great bar snacks you get in 'Sports Bars' in North America, although I have upped the ante somewhat. Rather than just crumb the zucchini and serve with a dipping sauce I make them with all the flavour stuck on—herbs, cheese, tomatoes, spices, the lot.

SUN-DRIED TOMATO CRUMBED FRIED ZUCCHINI STICKS

1 large zucchini (courgette)
2 free-range eggs
120 g (4¼ oz/1 cup) panko crumbs
25 g (1 oz/¼ cup) freshly grated parmesan cheese
100 g (3½ oz) sun-dried tomatoes
olive oil, for shallow-frying

75 g (2⅔ oz/½ cup) plain (all-purpose) flour
½ teaspoon ground oregano
½ teaspoon dried rosemary
½ teaspoon dried basil flakes
½ teaspoon salt
¼ teaspoon freshly ground black pepper

Preheat the oven to 160°C (315°F) (fan-forced 140°C/275°F).

Wash the zucchini then pat dry with paper towel. Trim the ends, then cut the zucchini in half so you have 2 long round pieces. Take one of the halves and cut it in half lengthways and then cut each half lengthways again into 4 pieces or wedges. You should have 8 pieces or wedges. Repeat with the other half so you end up with 16 pieces from one large zucchini.

Crack the eggs into a bowl and beat until well combined. Tip the panko crumbs onto a plate and mix through the grated cheese. Use a paper towel to soak the excess oil off the tomatoes, then finely chop and add to the panko crumbs. Gently rub the crumbs between your fingers until the tomatoes are evenly combined through the crumbs. This will take a couple of minutes. Set aside.

Pour some olive oil into a frying pan, about 1 cm (½ in) deep, then heat over medium–high heat.

Combine the flour, herbs, salt and pepper in a plastic bag. Add the zucchini and give it a really good shake to cover the zucchini sticks well. Working in batches, remove the zucchini from the bag, shake off the excess flour and place in the egg mixture. Completely coat each stick with egg, then place in the crumb mix. Cover with the crumbs and gently squeeze the sticks to firmly coat. Remove from the crumbs and put on a plate. Repeat with the remaining zucchini.

When the oil is shimmering hot, carefully put 6–8 zucchini sticks into the pan to cook. If you have cut them in wedges they will have three sides—two flat sides and one rounded side with skin, so after 1–1½ minutes turn the zucchini to cook another surface, then repeat after 1½ minutes, turning to cook the third side. Once all the sides are golden and crispy remove from the pan and drain on paper towel on a tray in the warm oven while you cook the remaining sticks.

To serve, stack on a plate and eat!

Makes 16 pieces

NOTE
You could serve with a dipping sauce or a chilli mayo if you want but with all of the spices, the sun-dried tomato and the cheese you don't really need to!

》》》》》》》》》》》》》》》》》》》》》》》》
TIP
You can make the zucchini sticks ahead of time. Once all have been crumbed put them on a plate, cover with plastic wrap and refrigerate until you want to cook them. They will last 2–3 days in the fridge.
》》》》》》》》》》》》》》》》》》》》》》》》

WARNING: Once you make this dish you will be hooked and need to make it again. Once you start eating it you won't be able to stop until it is all gone, in which case you will immediately want to make another batch. Don't say I didn't warn you. In my mind this is the perfect beer snack—sweet, salty, spicy and simply delicious.

SWEET PORK JERKY

2 tablespoons peanut butter

125 ml (4 fl oz/½ cup) tamari or soy sauce

2 teaspoons sambal oelek (3 if you want it hotter)

½ large or 1 small mango, pulped

2 teaspoons caster (superfine) sugar

1 teaspoon garlic powder

1 piece pickled pork* (about 700 g/1 lb 9 oz)

Put all the ingredients except the pork in a saucepan over medium heat. Bring to a simmer and stir well to combine. Simmer for a couple of minutes, until the sugar has dissolved, then remove from the heat and transfer into a large bowl or container. Set the marinade aside to cool completely.

Meanwhile, trim off any fat or membrane left on the pickled pork. Cut the meat across the grain into 3 cm (1¼ in) thick steaks. Put the steaks in the freezer until they are almost frozen. (Using part-frozen pork will make it easier to cut into nice even, thin strips of meat.)

Put one part-frozen pork steak on your work surface with the top of the pork facing your knife hand and cut into 2–3 mm (about ⅛ in) slices. You'll need a sharp knife for this. (Cutting along what was the top of the pork means you are cutting along the grain, or with the grain, which will help keep the jerky tender.) Remove another steak from the freezer and repeat.

Place the meat in the marinade and give it a really good mix to coat well. Cover with plastic wrap or a tight-fitting lid if using a plastic container and refrigerate for 3 days. Give the pork a mix twice a day—once in the morning when you get up and just before you go to bed.

Preheat the oven to 90°C (195°F) (fan-forced 70°C/150°F).

Remove the meat from the marinade and lay the pieces flat on several layers of paper towel. Place more layers of paper towel on top and press firmly to soak up the excess marinade. (The flavour is in the meat now and you do not want the meat wet when you put it in the oven to dry, as it may steam the meat and make it tough.) Lay the meat out on wire racks, well apart, and place in the oven, leaving the door slightly ajar so the air can circulate. It will take about 3–4 hours for the meat to dry, depending on how thick you ended up cutting the meat, what the temperature is outside and how your oven works. The meat should be dry but pliable and you should be able to tear it in half with your hands.

Eat! Or, if you have amazing willpower, the pork jerky can be stored in an airtight container with a paper towel folded in the bottom for up to 3 months.

Feeds 6

NOTE

You can buy pickled pork from your butcher or you can ask them to pickle it for you. It is basically pork put in a brine of salt, sugar, vinegar, spices and water. Tell them you want a 700 g (1 lb 9 oz) piece, however, it often comes in pieces around 1.3–1.7 kg (3 lb–3 lb 12 oz). Just follow the instructions in the recipe regarding cutting and portioning it and then you will have a batch in the freezer ready to go when you feel the urge to make another batch.

Haloumi seems to be all the rage at the moment and for good reason—it is simply delicious! Most bars and cafés serve up a grilled haloumi dish in some form or other as it makes for a fantastic snack. Due to the way it is made it will not melt and lose its shape when you cook it, so it is perfect for spicing up and throwing on the barbecue hotplate. You could grill it, cut it up and throw it in a salad, you could cut it into cubes and stuff it inside meatballs, you could finely dice it and throw it in a lamb stew! Or you could keep it simple and follow the recipe below ...

SMOKY SPICED HALOUMI

35 g (1¼ oz/¼ cup) plain (all-purpose) flour
2 tablespoons Smokey Tomatina spice mix*
250 g (9 oz) haloumi cheese

olive oil, for frying
1 lemon, cut into wedges

Put the flour in a plastic bag with the Smokey Tomatina and give it a good shake to mix together. Cut the haloumi into 3–5 mm (⅛–¼ in) thick pieces (or to your liking) then put in the bag and give it a good shake to coat well—the cheese should become orange from the Smokey Tomatina mix.

Heat the olive oil in a frying pan over medium heat or on your barbecue hotplate. Give the haloumi a bit of a shake to get rid of the excess flour and then put into the frying pan or onto the barbecue. Cook for about 4 minutes and then check it to see if it is developing a nice caramel colour and crust. If not, leave for another couple of minutes and then turn when the haloumi is nicely coloured. Cook the other side until coloured and crisp—all up about 10–15 minutes depending on how hot your cooker is.

Serve on a plate with the lemon wedges, and of course a good beer.

Makes about 7 pieces

NOTE: Smokey Tomatina is a wonderful mix of spice, smoke, salt and sweetness that you should be able to find on the internet. If you have trouble finding it, you could also go down to your local farmers' market and check out what spice mix is on offer—just have a taste before you buy to find the one that works best for your tastebuds. Or why not try making your own spice mix—just combine ½ teaspoon each of garlic powder, salt, chilli powder, smoky paprika, ground cumin powder, dried oregano or oregano powder and lemon pepper.

»»»»»»»»»»»»»»»»»»»»»
TIP
Haloumi is quite a salty cheese so you shouldn't need to season the flour with any salt—however taste the cheese first to see if it is salty enough for you and remember that cooking the cheese tends to accent the saltiness even more.
»»»»»»»»»»»»»»»»»»»»»

Sometimes making hummus seems to be a dark art as it is all about the balance between the chickpeas, tahini, lemon juice, garlic and salt. I make this quite often and love it, but even though I follow the recipe below, at times it needs a little more of something or other. Perhaps it's just that my tastebuds are in a different mood from one week to the next, I don't know, but the point is don't be afraid to play with this a little and keep tasting it to get the balance right.

HUMMUS

1 tin (400 g/14 oz) chickpeas, plus 2 tablespoons of
    reserved liquid from the tin
1 garlic clove, crushed
3 tablespoons tahini paste*

60 ml (2 fl oz/¼ cup) lemon juice
salt and freshly ground black pepper
⅛ teaspoon ground cumin
⅛ teaspoon chilli powder (optional, but I love it)

Put the chickpeas and chickpea liquid in a blender or food processor and blend for 1 minute. Scrape down the side and blend again for 1 minute. Add the garlic and tahini paste, and blend for another minute. Stop and scrape down the side and then blend again for another minute. With the blender running, gradually add the lemon juice, stop and scrape down the side again, season with salt and pepper, add the cumin and chilli, if using, then give it all a final blend. Taste for seasoning and adjust if needed, but if you follow this recipe it shouldn't need any more seasoning. I would put a little more cumin and chilli in for my taste, say ¼ teaspoon of each, but for the sake of the book I have been easy-handed.

Tip out into a bowl and cover with plastic wrap until you are ready to serve. It will last in the fridge for 3–5 days. Serve with some good quality corn chips (see tip).

FEEDS 4–6

NOTE: You can find tahini at health food shops or the health food aisle at your local supermarket.

》》》》》》》》》》》》》》》》》》》》》》》》
TIP
I love corn chips, but you do need to look at the ingredients list before you buy them as some are cooked using palm oil which is really not very good for us, or the environment.
》》》》》》》》》》》》》》》》》》》》》》》》

Back in the old days when I was a student at the Australian Ballet School I used to work at the local Mexican fast-food restaurant and the trick to good nachos, I discovered, was to set the corn chips in the beans so they stood up like cathedrals, allowing the toppings to fall in between and give you a lovely taste surprise with each mouthful. Let's face it, there's nothing worse than flat, soggy nachos with all the cheese on top and nothing underneath! So take the time to make corn chip cathedrals and people will think you're a genius!

NACHOS EXTRAORDINAIRE

2 tablespoons olive oil
1 small onion, finely diced
1 fresh jalapeño chilli, finely diced
1 garlic clove, finely chopped
½ teaspoon ground cumin
1 teaspoon Mexican chilli powder
1 teaspoon smoky paprika
150 g (5½ oz) minced (ground) pork
150 g (5½ oz) lean minced (ground) beef
1 tomato, diced
2 tablespoons store-bought black bean and
    chipotle salsa

2 tablespoons store-bought roasted tomatillo salsa
6 tablespoons chopped pickled jalapeño chillies
salt and freshly ground black pepper
½ tin (220 g/7¾ oz) Mexican refried beans
1 tin (420 g/15 oz) Mexican pinto beans or
    kidney beans
1 large packet good quality plain or lightly salted
    corn chips
150 g (5½ oz/1½ cups) grated cheddar or Monterey
    Jack cheese
1 large avocado, roughly mashed
125 g (4½ oz/½ cup) sour cream

Preheat the oven to 200°C (400°F) (fan-forced 180°/350°F).

Heat the olive oil in a large frying pan over medium–high heat. Add the onion and fresh jalapeño and cook until the onion is translucent, then add the garlic and cook for a couple more minutes. Add the cumin, Mexican chilli powder and paprika, and fry until fragrant and well combined with the onion. Increase the heat to high and add the pork and beef. Use a wooden spoon to break up the meat and mix well, then continue to cook until the meat is evenly browned. Next, add the tomato, chipotle salsa, tomatillo salsa and 2 tablespoons of the chopped jalapeños, reduce the heat to medium and cook for several minutes. Taste and add salt and pepper as required. Remove the pan from the heat and set aside.

Spread the refried beans over the bottom of an ovenproof casserole dish, about 1 cm (½ in) thick. Spread about a third of the pinto beans on top of the refried beans, then place your corn chips, upright, into the bean mix (yes, I do it one by one—you may think I'm mad—but the results are worth it!). Sprinkle the rest of the Mexican beans over the top, followed by 2 tablespoons of the chopped jalapeños, then the meat mixture—making sure it falls down the crevices. Sprinkle the remaining chopped jalapeños over the meat, then sprinkle over the grated cheese. Put the dish in the oven and bake until the cheese has melted and begins to colour. Put the mashed avocado over one side of the nachos and the sour cream on the other and dig in.

Feeds 4–6

I was lucky enough to have a week-long gig in Buenos Aires a couple of years ago and on one of my free afternoons I had a good walkabout around town—it's a big town! Down a small side street I stumbled upon an empanaderia (a bakery or restaurant that specialises in making empanadas). It was a very unassuming place but, as you would expect, the empanadas were out-of-this-world good. From that moment on I have been bitten by the empanada bug. There are many styles throughout the Americas depending on nationality and township—this recipe is based on the Argentinian style, although to make it more authentic it should have some hard-boiled egg chopped through it.

ARGENTINE EMPANADAS

2 tablespoons olive oil
2 tablespoons butter
1 red onion, halved and sliced
1 teaspoon paprika
1 teaspoon cayenne pepper
½ teaspoon ground cumin
600 g (1 lb 5 oz) beef shin, cut into 3 cm (1¼ in) cubes
2 tablespoons sherry vinegar
500 ml (17 fl oz/2 cups) beef stock (although you may not use it all)
45 g (1⅔ oz/¼ cup) sultanas (golden raisins)
85 g (3 oz/½ cup) Spanish stuffed green olives, roughly chopped
1 cinnamon stick
salt and freshly ground black pepper
2 potatoes, finely diced
110 g (3¾ oz/¾ cup) frozen peas, defrosted
1 free-range egg, beaten

Dough

1 free-range egg
1 free-range egg white
1 teaspoon vinegar
450 g (1 lb/3 cups) plain (all-purpose) flour
1 teaspoon salt
3 tablespoons lard

Preheat the oven to 170°C (325°F) (fan-forced 150°C/300°F).

Heat the olive oil and butter in a flameproof casserole dish over medium heat. Add the onion and gently fry until translucent and caramelised. Add the paprika, cayenne pepper and cumin, and cook for a couple of minutes to allow the fragrance to develop. Increase the heat to high, add the meat and cook, stirring constantly with a wooden spoon, for about 5 minutes until all the meat is well browned, then deglaze the pan with the sherry vinegar. Add 250 ml (9 fl oz/1 cup) of the stock, the sultanas, olives and cinnamon, and bring to the boil. Turn off the heat and taste for seasoning, adding salt and pepper as needed. Put a sheet of baking paper over the meat, then cover with the lid and transfer to the oven. »→

◀◀◀

Cook for 1 hour, then remove the baking paper, add the potato and give it all a good stir. Put the baking paper back over the meat and potato, cover with the lid and cook for another hour, checking on the liquid after 30 minutes and adding a little extra stock if required—enough to keep everything moist but not swimming.

After the meat has been cooking for 2 hours, remove the cinnamon stick then add the peas and stir them through. The residual heat of the sauce will cook the peas so you do not need to return the dish to the oven. The meat should be tender enough that if you push down with the back of a wooden spoon it falls apart—do this to all of the meat, but be careful not to smash the other ingredients. Allow the meat mixture to cool completely.

While the meat cools make your dough. Put the egg, egg white, vinegar and 125 ml (4 fl oz/½ cup) of water in a bowl and use a whisk to combine well. Put the flour and salt in a food processor and combine. Gradually add the lard, a little at a time, and pulse to combine. Gradually add the egg mixture, blending, until it forms a ball.

Tip the dough onto a lightly floured work surface and knead it for a couple of minutes, just so it comes together, then form it into a ball, wrap in plastic wrap and refrigerate for at least 1 hour.

Increase the oven temperature to 200°C (400°F) (fan-forced 180°C/350°F).

Cut the dough in half, cover and put one half back in the fridge while you make the first round of empanadas. Roll the dough out 3–4 mm (about ⅛ in) thick and, using a teacup saucer as a guide, cut out rounds approximately 12 cm (4½ in) in diameter to make about four rounds, then reroll the dough scraps and cut out another two rounds and repeat with the scraps to get another round out of it. Place 2 tablespoons of the cooled meat mixture into the centre of each round, brush a little beaten egg around the edge, then fold over and pinch the edges together. Use a fork to impress a pattern around the joined edges or you can crimp and fold the edges up and over each other. Repeat with the remaining dough—depending on how good you were at rolling out the squished up dough you should have somewhere between 14 and 16 empanadas.

Line two baking trays with baking paper and evenly space the empanadas on top. Use a pastry brush to brush the empanadas with a little of the beaten egg to glaze, then bake for 25–30 minutes or until the empanadas are golden brown. Serve warm with a glass of wine or a craft ale.

Makes about 16

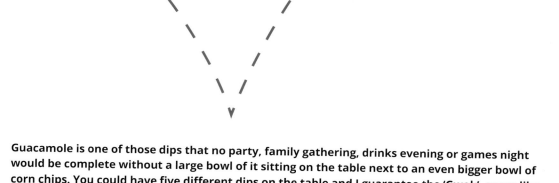

Guacamole is one of those dips that no party, family gathering, drinks evening or games night would be complete without a large bowl of it sitting on the table next to an even bigger bowl of corn chips. You could have five different dips on the table and I guarantee the 'Gwok', as we like to call it, will be the first to be finished. My daughter makes hers slightly differently from mine (everyone has their own little tweaks and quirks), but if you ask me, mine is the winner.

GUACAMOLE

2–3 large ripe avocados
1 garlic clove, crushed
1 small red onion, finely chopped
1 red bird's-eye chilli, finely chopped
1 tablespoon finely chopped pickled
   jalapeño chillies

2 tablespoons store-bought mild or hot salsa
juice of ½ lime (about 2 teaspoons)
1–2 teaspoons Tabasco sauce
2 tablespoons finely chopped coriander
   (cilantro) leaves
pinch of salt

Cut the avocados in half, remove the stones and then spoon the flesh out and put it in a bowl, discarding the skin. Mash the avocado with a fork or potato masher. Add all of the other ingredients except the salt and mix well so that everything is well combined. Taste and season with salt, then taste again and adjust accordingly.

Serve in a large bowl with plenty of corn chips for dipping.

Feeds 4–6

Fajita is a traditional Mexican ranch dish thought to have originated in the 1930s. Mexican cowboys had to be fed while they were tending the cattle, but the ranchers didn't want to use good, sellable meat to feed them, so instead throw-away cuts were used—in this case, skirt steak. The meat was marinated to make it more tender and then grilled directly on the coals, or on a grill over coals or an open fire, and was served on a corn tortilla with the usual Mexican-style accompaniments. Nowadays, you can buy fajita seasoning and corn tortillas at major grocery stores and make your own fajita using chicken, pork, fish, lamb, beef, goat or even kangaroo if you want. It is a great dish—easy to make, although it does have a number of components—and is ideal for feeding a hungry group. For something different, I've used goat meat.

GOAT FAJITA

1 goat leg (about 700 g/1 lb 9 oz deboned),
    cut into thin steaks across the grain
2 tablespoons olive oil
1 red onion, thinly sliced
1 red capsicum (pepper), cut into strips
10 warm tortillas, to serve
1 tin (420 g/15 oz) kidney beans or Mexican pinto
    beans, drained and rinsed, to serve
150 g (5½ oz/1½ cups) grated cheddar cheese,
    to serve
90 g (3¼ oz/2 cups) sliced lettuce, to serve

Marinade
330 ml (11¼ fl oz/1⅓ cups) can Wild Turkey and
    Cola (Kentucky-style bourbon and cola)
2 garlic cloves, peeled and smashed with the flat
    of a knife
2 red chillies, chopped

Simple Guacamole
2 large or 3 small ripe avocados
½ red onion, finely diced
2 garlic cloves, finely diced
juice of 1 lime (about 1 tablespoon)
½ teaspoon salt
½ teaspoon freshly ground black pepper

Pico De Gallo
2 large tomatoes
¾ red onion, diced
1 tablespoon chopped pickled jalapeño chillies
2 tablespoons chopped coriander (cilantro) leaves
1 tablespoon olive oil
juice of 1 lime (about 1 tablespoon)
salt and freshly ground black pepper

Salsa Roja
2 tomatoes
3 red chillies
1 garlic clove
¼ red onion
1 tablespoon chopped coriander (cilantro) leaves
pinch of salt

Beetroot Chutney
60 ml (2 fl oz/¼ cup) olive oil
2 beetroot (beet), peeled and grated
3 spring onions (scallions), chopped
2 garlic cloves, thinly sliced
1 red chilli, finely chopped
60 ml (2 fl oz/ ¼ cup) sherry vinegar
125 ml (4 fl oz/½ cup) dry red wine
1 tablespoon brown sugar
salt and freshly ground black pepper ⟫➞

←◀◀

First, marinate the goat. Put the Wild Turkey and Cola in a large bowl or container with the garlic and chillies. Add the goat and stir to coat. Cover with plastic wrap or the container lid and set aside to marinate for at least an hour or overnight in the fridge, or for as long as it takes you to prepare the accompaniments.

To make the simple guacamole, cut the avocados in half, remove the seed and scoop the fruit out into a bowl and mash. Add the rest of the ingredients and mix through the avocado so they are well combined. Taste for seasoning and adjust accordingly. This is a very simple guacamole—and delicious—it takes into account all the other accompaniments. Set aside, covered, until needed.

To make the pico de gallo, score a shallow cross in the base of each tomato. Put in a heatproof bowl and cover with boiling water. Leave for 30 seconds, then transfer to cold water and peel the skin away from the cross. To seed, cut the tomato in half and scoop out the seeds with a teaspoon. Dice the tomato flesh and place in a large bowl. Add the onion, chopped jalapeño, coriander, olive oil and lime juice and give it all a very good mix. Taste for seasoning and add salt and pepper as needed. Set aside.

To make the salsa roja, roughly chop all the ingredients except the salt, put in a food processor or blender, season with salt and then blend until very well combined and smooth. Pour into a bowl and set aside.

This is not really a Mexican thing, but I picked up some great organic beetroots and spring onions one day and just had to cook them up to make a chutney, and they worked well with goat. Heat the olive oil in a frying pan over medium–high heat. Add the beetroot, spring onion, garlic and chilli and cook for about 5 minutes, stirring occasionally. Add the sherry vinegar, wine and sugar, and mix together so that the sugar dissolves, then simmer gently until the beetroot is cooked. If it becomes too dry before the beetroot is cooked, add a little more red wine or water to keep it moist.

When all the accompaniments are prepared, cook the goat. Heat a large frying pan or chargrill pan over medium–high heat. Add the olive oil and when hot add the onion and capsicum and fry, stirring frequently, for several minutes until the onion is translucent and the capsicum is softened. Remove the meat from the marinade, shake off the excess liquid, then add to the hot pan and fry, stirring constantly, until it is just cooked and has taken on a little colour.

You may need to cook the goat in batches until it is all done. Better still, cook the meat on a barbecue—that way you will get some nice charring and also some of the smoky character that the cowboys would have had when they cooked their meat on the open fire. If you use a barbecue, cook the onion and capsicum separately and add it to the meat when it is all cooked.

Tip the goat mixture onto a plate and serve. The idea is to tear a tortilla in half, spread a teaspoon of the guacamole over it, place some goat, onion and capsicum on top, a little pico de gallo, some salsa roja, a few beans and a sprinkle of cheese. Do the same with the other half, but maybe use some goat, beetroot chutney, salsa roja and lettuce. Make it up as you go along and have fun with it.

Feeds 4–6

I love a good quality gin with some tonic and a slice of lemon—three simple ingredients combined to make something exceptional. Mind you, some gins are made with ten or more ingredients by way of herbs and spices. There are also a few more ingredients in this gin concoction, but once combined—the marinade, the quail and the smokiness from cooking on a barbecue—it's equally as exceptional as my gin and tonic.

GRILLED GIN-MARINATED QUAIL

4 quails (about 600 g/1 lb 5 oz each)
1 garlic clove, crushed
1 red chilli, finely chopped
1 spring onion (scallion), thinly sliced
60 ml (2 fl oz/¼ cup) gin

juice of ¼ lime (about 1 teaspoon)
1 tablespoon finely chopped basil
1 tablespoon soy sauce
¼ teaspoon freshly ground black pepper
¼ teaspoon sugar

Wash the quails under cold water, then pat dry with paper towels. Use kitchen scissors to cut down either side of the backbone, remove and discard. Place a quail, breast side up on your work surface and act like you are going to give it CPR, using your palms to flatten the quail out. Using a sharp knife, make three or four shallow cuts over the quail—this will help the marinade to penetrate.

Mix all the remaining ingredients together in a baking tray or small glass baking dish. Place the quails in the tray and rub the marinade all over the birds. Cover with plastic wrap and place in the fridge for at least 2 hours to marinate.

Preheat the barbecue grill to medium–high.

Remove the quail from the marinade, shake off the excess liquid and place on the grill. Cook, skin down side, for about 8 minutes, then turn and cook, bone side down, for 8 minutes more. Reduce the heat to medium, turn the quail and cook for another 5 minutes, then turn and cook for a final 5 minutes to finish cooking—you will know the quail is cooked when the joints move freely and can be pulled away easily from the body.

Serve the quail with whatever you fancy. I like to serve it with the soft salad on page 96 and some smoky spiced haloumi from page 55.

Feeds 4

I love a good beer-battered piece of fish, as long as you use a good quality craft beer, but equally I love a good spicy piece of fish to go with my glass of good quality beer. The rice flour in this recipe helps to hold the spices to the fish and also create a crispy exterior. It works well with prawns too, hint hint!

CAJUN LING

1 large long rock ling fillet (about 600 g/1 lb 5 oz)
2 teaspoons lemon pepper
2 tablespoons rice flour
1 teaspoon chilli powder
1 teaspoon Cajun spice mix

1 teaspoon smoky paprika
½ teaspoon chipotle powder
½ teaspoon salt
olive oil, for shallow-frying

Cut the ling fillet lengthways down the middle so you end up with one long round thick fillet and one long flat or flap of fillet. Reserve the flap for another day. Take the long thick round fillet and cut it in half to make two equal lengths, then cut each half lengthways down the middle to make four thick sausage-type fillets.

Mix the remaining ingredients, except the olive oil, together in a plastic bag. Add the fish and shake to coat the fillets evenly. Remove the fish from the bag, shake off the excess flour and set aside on a plate.

Pour some olive oil into a large frying pan, about 1 cm (½ in) deep, then heat over medium–high heat until you can see it shimmering. Carefully lay the fish in the pan and shallow-fry, turning several times until golden and cooked through. By turning the fillets over you can control the heat and cooking speed of each side so as not to burn the batter and allow the fillets to cook evenly. You will need to reduce the heat to medium after about 3–4 minutes of cooking. Transfer onto paper towel to drain.

Serve with lemon wedges or chilli mayonnaise (see note).

Feeds 2

NOTE

To make chilli mayonnaise, combine 120 g (4¼ oz/½ cup) whole-egg mayonnaise with ½ tablespoon chilli paste (to give it some kick), in a bowl.

What can I say about this dish—super cheap, super easy and super delicious! You should have all these spices in your pantry as part of your basic supply, and now here is a good reason to make sure you do.

BARBECUED LAMB RIBS

1 teaspoon fennel seeds
1 teaspoon cumin seeds
1 teaspoon garlic powder
1 teaspoon celery salt
1 teaspoon sweet paprika

1 teaspoon dried rosemary
1 teaspoon dried thyme
½ teaspoon salt
½ teaspoon freshly ground black pepper
3 trimmed lamb rib racks (about 1 kg/2 lb 4 oz)

Preheat the barbecue grill to medium–high.

Dry-fry the fennel and cumin seeds in a small frying pan over high heat until they begin to lightly smoke. Turn off the heat and tip the seeds into your mortar then use the pestle to grind them into a powder. Add the rest of the ingredients, except the lamb, and grind together well to make a rub. Generously cover the lamb ribs with the rub then place the ribs, fat/meat side down, onto the hot barbecue grill. The fat from the ribs will render out and baste the ribs, but you do need to keep an eye on them in case you get flare-ups (that is, the fat catches fire). If this happens, move the ribs out of the fire to another part of the grill and continue cooking. Don't worry if the ribs get a little charred from the flames, that's all part of the theatre and the taste of a barbie! After about 5–7 minutes turn the ribs over and cook for another 5–7 minutes and then remove from the heat.

Cut the racks into separate ribs and pile them high on a plate so people can help themselves. Watch mates carefully, though—once they start eating these they won't be able to stop and you may not get any.

I love barbecued lamb ribs on their own, but they're also great with a tomato chilli chutney to dip them in and some 'slaw (see page 83)—which is great with barbecued everything!

Makes about 21 ribs

Pulled pork American-barbecue style is all the rage at the moment, however, in my house it has been all the rage since I first started doing smoked pork, brisket and ribs way back in 2004 after living in Canada while working on a Will Smith movie. (I just had to drop that in!) Slow-cooking in your oven or smoking on your barbecue is super easy and super simple, it just takes time. The good thing is once it's in the oven you can go shopping, see a couple of movies, do the vacuuming and mow the lawn. If you are smoking the meat you do need to add wood chips every half hour or so, so you are not quite as free—you can't go out and see a movie but you can still mow the lawn and do other stuff. One thing's for sure though, once you've made this it will become a weekend staple so your lawn should look pretty good.

PULLED PORK

1 whole pork neck (about 1.5 kg/3 lb 5 oz)
2 tablespoons garlic powder
2 tablespoons smoky paprika
2 tablespoons fennel powder
2 tablespoons chilli powder
2 tablespoons salt

2 tablespoons onion powder
1 tablespoon sage powder
1 tablespoon freshly ground black pepper
4 tablespoons brown sugar
smoky barbecue sauce (see page 82)

Oven version

Preheat the oven to 120°C (235°F) (fan-force 100°C/200°F).

Take the pork out of the fridge and leave it on your work surface to come up to room temperature. Combine all the other ingredients, except the smoky barbecue sauce, in a bowl and mix together well. Rub the spice mix all over the pork neck so it is well coated. Place the pork in a roasting tin and cook until it reaches an internal temperature of 85–90°C (185–195°F)—depending on the size of your piece of pork this could take anywhere from 6 to 10 hours. Do not be tempted to pull it out before it reaches an internal temperature of at least 85°C (185°F) which is when the proteins in the meat will break down and make the pork melt-in-your-mouth tender. Remove the pork from the oven, tightly wrap in foil and then leave to rest for an hour or so. Reserve any cooking liquid in the roasting tin.

Remove the foil, being careful to capture any juices, and set that aside. Use two forks to shred the meat and then place the meat in a bowl, giving it a good mix. Add the collected juice from the roasting tin and the foil wrapping back into the meat along with a generous squirt of my smoky barbecue sauce and mix again.

To serve, put the bowl of pulled pork on the table with either some bap rolls or just some corn chips. For a slap-up party experience, add sides of salsa, guacamole (page 63), 'slaw (page 83) and more of my smoky barbecue sauce! You could also add this to nachos (page 59) for an even bigger flavour hit.

Barbecue version

For true barbecue style you can smoke this on a kettle barbecue very easily. You can buy hickory wood chips from your hardware or barbecue store. Soak a large bowl of wood chips in warm water for an hour or so before using. It is good if you use one of those heat-bead barbecue starters which you can get from the same place you buy the wood chips. Place about 15–20 heat-bead briquettes in the starter and follow the instructions to light the briquettes. Once they are covered in white ash transfer about 10 into one of the side baskets of your barbecue, place an oven thermometer on the grill away from the briquettes, put the lid on and let the barbecue heat up for 20 minutes. Check the temperature on the gauge—hopefully it will be about 100°C (200°F), if not, add one or two more hot briquettes from the starter to help bring the temperature up. If it is over, say 110°C (225°F) that is still okay—when you put the pork in it should absorb that heat in the first 30 minutes. Ideally, you want the temperature in the barbecue to hover around the 100°C (200°F) mark for the entire cook, so keep some coals hot in the starter and add when the heat begins to drop.

Cover your room temperature pork with the rub, then place the pork on the grill away from the heat of the briquettes. Place a handful of the wood chips (shake off the excess water first) directly onto the burning coals and put the lid on with the air vent open and on the opposite side from the coals. This allows the smoke to rise up and roll over the meat as it makes its way out through the vent. Repeat the process of adding wood chips every 25–30 minutes. Cooking time will depend on the size of your piece of pork, the ambient temperature, how windy it is and what sort of mood you are in, so the best bit of advice I can give is patience—it will be ready when it's ready and that is when it reaches 85–90°C (185–195°F) internally. Remove from the barbecue and wrap tightly in foil for an hour or so, then pull apart.

Feeds 6–8

Don't be put off by the fact you are marinating your chicken in fish sauce! Yes, it seems weird and smells a little funky, BUT the end result is absolutely delicious and, no, it doesn't taste like fish sauce when it's cooked. This is a great one-handed snack—the tenderloins are super tasty and crispy—perfect with a beer and the footy on. That said, I'm a rugby league man!

CRISPY ASIAN-STYLE CHICKEN TENDERLOINS

16 chicken tenderloins (about 800 g/1 lb 12 oz)
80 g (2¾ oz/½ cup) rice flour
75 g (2⅔ oz/½ cup) plain (all-purpose) flour
30 g (1 oz/¼ cup) rice crumbs
vegetable oil, for deep-frying

Marinade
½ red onion, finely diced
1 lemongrass stem, white part only, crushed
2 garlic cloves, crushed
2 small red chillies, finely chopped
½ teaspoon Chinese five-spice mix
½ teaspoon cayenne pepper
½ teaspoon ground coriander
½ teaspoon freshly ground black pepper
1 tablespoon caster (superfine) sugar
juice of ½ lime (about 2 teaspoons)
125 ml (4 fl oz/½ cup) fish sauce

Combine the marinade ingredients in a large non-metallic bowl or container. Add the chicken and stir to coat. Cover with plastic wrap or the container lid and set aside to marinate for at least 30 minutes or, better still, a couple of hours in the fridge.

Combine the flours and rice crumbs in a bowl.

Preheat the oven to 160°C (315°F) (fan-forced 140°C/275°F).

Put enough vegetable oil in a deep frying pan or a wok to deep-fry the chicken and put over high heat.

While the oil comes up to temperature, remove the chicken from the fridge and, working in batches, four at a time, shake off the excess marinade, dredge them in the flour, coating well, then shake off the excess flour. When the oil is shimmering hot, carefully place the chicken, a few at a time, in the oil and deep-fry until crispy and golden brown. Use tongs to carefully remove the chicken from the hot oil and transfer onto a baking tray lined with paper towel then place in the warm oven while you cook the remaining chicken batches. Serve!

Makes 16 pieces

Ras el hanout is a Moroccan spice blend that is considered the king of spice mixes and it can contain more than thirty different types of spices. Some blends have even been known to have up to 100 different spices. It is great on anything barbecued! You can buy this spice blend in your local gourmet deli or at your local supermarket. I made this recipe for my TV show *Mercurio's Menu* using some beautiful products from the town and area of Cobram in Victoria. If you can find their produce then use it, but don't stress if you can't—just use what you have. The main thing is the ras el hanout.

MOROCCAN LAMB WITH CACTUS SALSA

1 lamb leg, bone in (about 1.5 kg/3 lb 5 oz) (I used saltbush lamb for this recipe)

2 garlic cloves, halved then cut into three wedges per half

1 teaspoon salt

½ teaspoon freshly ground black pepper

chilli oil or extra virgin olive oil

80 g (2¾ oz) ras el hanout spice mix

Cactus Salsa

5 roma (plum) tomatoes, peeled, seeded and diced

1 small red onion, finely diced

15 g (½ oz/½ cup) chopped coriander (cilantro) leaves

2 tablespoons chopped pickled jalapeño chillies

95 g (3¼ oz/½ cup) cactus, peeled and diced*

100 g (3½ oz/⅔ cup) crumbled feta cheese

salt and freshly ground black pepper

juice of ½ lime (about 2 teaspoons)

2 tablespoons lemon–lime oil or extra virgin olive oil

Preheat the barbecue or oven to about 200°C (400°F) (fan-forced 180°C/350°F).

Use a small sharp knife to stab the leg of lamb and insert a wedge of garlic into the hole. Repeat this using all of the garlic, evenly distributing across the lamb leg. Season with the salt and pepper, then drizzle the chilli oil over the lamb (you can use extra virgin olive oil if you want). Generously coat the entire leg with the ras el hanout spice mix, rubbing it into the meat. Put the lamb on the barbecue and cook with the lid down using indirect heat, or in the oven, for 1½ hours until the internal temperature of the meat is about 58–61°C (135–140°F). Medium–rare will be 58° and 61°C will be closer to medium.

Meanwhile, make the cactus salsa. Put the tomato, onion, coriander, jalepeño, cactus and feta in a large bowl and mix together well. Season with a little salt and black pepper, squeeze the lime over, then drizzle in the lemon–lime oil. Mix again, taste for seasoning and adjust as needed.

Remove the lamb from the barbecue or oven and rest on a cutting board for 5–10 minutes before carving.

To serve, carve big slices of lamb and put them into long hot dog rolls that have been split open. Spoon a generous amount of salsa over the lamb and eat!

Feeds 8–10

NOTE

You can buy cactus in tins or jars, but if you can't find it, use raw diced zucchini (courgettes) instead.

I love pies and, even more, I love to make my own pies. Yes, it is a bit of a labour of love, but the end result and the smiles on people's faces when you serve them up is well worth it, not to mention they are super delicious. I love doing the good old Sunday cook-up and then vacuum-packing the pies and freezing them for later use. The best thing is when I clean the freezer out later on and find a long-lost pie up the back—it's like winning a trophy!

LAMB AND ROSEMARY PIES

100 ml (3½ fl oz) olive oil, plus extra for greasing

1 red onion, diced

2 garlic cloves, crushed

2 carrots, finely chopped

2 parsnips, finely chopped

2 tablespoons chopped rosemary

75 g (2⅔ oz/½ cup) plain (all-purpose) flour

¼ teaspoon salt

¼ teaspoon white pepper

850 g (1 lb 14 oz) deboned lamb leg or shoulder, cut into 2 cm (¾ in) cubes

125 ml (4 fl oz/½ cup) dry red wine

500 ml (17 fl oz/2 cups) vegetable stock

1 tablespoon worcestershire sauce

1 teaspoon freshly ground black pepper

140 g (5 oz/1 cup) frozen peas

8 sheets shortcrust pastry (for the pie bottoms)

4 sheets puff pastry (for the pie lids)

1 free-range egg, beaten

poppy seeds (optional)

Place a flameproof casserole dish over medium–high heat, add 2 tablespoons of the olive oil and when hot add the onion and fry for 5 minutes. Add the garlic, carrot, parsnip and rosemary and fry for a further 10 minutes, stirring every few minutes. Remove from the heat, then remove the vegetables from the dish and set aside.

Put the flour, salt and white pepper in a plastic bag and mix to combine. Add the lamb to the bag and then shake to coat the meat evenly.

Return the casserole dish to the heat, add 2 more tablespoons of the olive oil and increase the heat to high. Shake the excess flour from the lamb and when the oil is hot, brown the lamb in two batches. Once the first batch is browned remove from the dish and add the remaining oil and brown the second batch of meat. Remove the second batch of browned meat and deglaze the pan with the red wine, scraping all the stuck-on bits off the base of the pan. Add the remaining flour from coating the lamb to the pan, stirring until well mixed. Add the stock and stir to combine. Return the cooked veggies and the browned meat to the dish, and ⟫⟶

◄-◄◄

mix well. Add the worcestershire sauce and black pepper, mix again, and bring to the boil, then reduce the heat to a simmer. Cover the top of the stew with a piece of baking paper that has been pre-cut to snuggly fit in the casserole, then place the lid on top. Simmer over very low heat for 1 hour and then check the dish—the lamb should be very tender and the sauce thick. Add the peas and mix through. If the sauce is too thick you can add a little stock or water to loosen it up, if it is too thin remove all the solids and increase the heat to reduce the sauce. Taste for seasoning and adjust as needed. Remove from the heat and set aside to cool.

Preheat the oven to 200°C (400°F) (fan-forced 180°C/350°F).

Grease eight individual pie tins (or two Texan muffin trays) with a little olive oil (see note). Cut out eight rounds from the shortcrust pastry—these will be the bottoms of your pies so make sure you cut a big enough circle to fit in your pie tin and up the sides with excess hanging over—I use a tea cup saucer as a guide. Make sure when you work the pastry into the pie tin that it is of uniform thickness all the way around. Fill your pie bases with the cold meat mixture and then cut out eight rounds from the puff pastry to make your lids—I use the pie tins as a guide. Brush the overhanging pastry with the beaten egg, then lay your lid on top of the pie, fold the bottom over the top and twist or crimp all the way around the edge with a fork to seal. Brush a little more of the egg over the top and then sprinkle with poppy seeds. Bake for 25–30 minutes or until golden. Remove from the oven and leave to cool for a few minutes before turning out and eating.

The lamb and rosemary mixture can also be used as a stew instead of making pies, served with some mashed potatoes. You could also add a side of steamed green beans, although there are plenty of vegetables in the stew already.

Makes 8

NOTE

I like to make different shaped pies so I often use normal pie tins, large Texan muffin tins and small springform cheesecake tins. The variety gives the pies a lovely rustic look when you serve them up to a group of people.
You can also top the lids with rosemary sprigs.

When I was living in America I was surprised and disappointed to find that sausage rolls don't exist there! Nor do they have them in Canada, they don't seem that common in the UK either, and I certainly haven't found them in Italy, Germany, Belgium, Greece, Holland, Switzerland, Japan or China. This is the rest of the world's loss—they are such a convenient snack, you can eat them with one hand and hold a beer in the other, and if you make them with a little thought they can actually be quite healthy. You can go the added distance and make your own pastry, but store-bought pastry (which I've used here) still does a brilliant job.

GOURMET SAUSAGE ROLLS

2 tablespoons olive oil, plus extra for frying
1 large red onion, finely diced
2 garlic cloves, finely chopped
1 large carrot, grated
1 large zucchini (courgette), grated
½ teaspoon finely chopped sage
1 tablespoon chopped flat-leaf (Italian) parsley
salt and freshly ground black pepper

500 g (1 lb 2 oz) minced (ground) beef
500 g (1 lb 2 oz) minced (ground) pork
1 free-range egg
2 tablespoons soy sauce
2 tablespoons sweet chilli sauce
30 g (1 oz/½ cup) panko breadcrumbs (optional)
4 sheets puff pastry
1 beaten free-range egg

Preheat the oven to 200°C (400°F) (fan-forced 180°C/350°F).

Heat the olive oil in a frying pan over medium–high heat, add the onion and cook gently for about 5 minutes. Add the garlic and cook for a couple of minutes, then add the carrot and zucchini, stir well to combine, and cook for 8 minutes, stirring occasionally. Add the herbs, season with salt and pepper, mix well, then transfer into a sieve and leave to cool and drain away any excess fluid.

Put the meats in a large bowl and mix well to combine, then add the egg, soy sauce, sweet chilli and salt and pepper, and mix for about 5 minutes until well combined. When the veggies are cool add to the meat and mix together well. Add the breadcrumbs, if using, and mix thoroughly.

Heat a little olive oil in a frying pan over high heat. Take a tablespoon of the meat and form it into a small patty and then add to the pan. Cook for about 4 minutes, turning occasionally until evenly browned and cooked through. When cooked, taste and adjust the seasoning of the uncooked mix as needed.

Lay a sheet of pastry on your work surface then shape some of the meat mixture on it in a long sausage the length of the pastry sheet and about 4 cm (1½ in) from the bottom edge. Roll up the pastry, brush the joining edge with a little of the beaten egg, then enclose the mince mixture, sealing it in. Cut along the bottom length of the roll, then cut the roll in half and place, seam side down, on a baking tray lined with baking paper. Repeat this process three more times with whole sheets of pastry, reserving the cut off pieces. Use the cut off pieces to make smaller rolls by turning the pastry sheet so that its length runs in the direction from the bottom of your work surface to the top. You can make two short rolls out of each cut off sheet. Repeat until all the mixture is used. You should end up with 16 sausage rolls.

Brush the tops of the sausage rolls with beaten egg and then cook for about 30–35 minutes or until golden brown. Because there is fresh vegetable in the mix you will get some liquid coming out of the rolls which can make the bottom of the pastry soggy. Remove the sausage rolls from the oven and put them on a clean baking tray lined with baking paper with the soggy bottoms facing up, put them back in the oven and cook for another 10 minutes so the pastry can dry out and crisp up. Remove the sausage rolls from the oven and leave to cool slightly (see note). Serve with tomato sauce or my smoky barbecue sauce (see page 82).

Makes 16

NOTE

These sausage rolls are also handy to freeze for another day. Cool completely, place them in zip-lock bags and freeze for up to 3 months. I have a home vacuum-pack machine which is great for sealing all sorts of prepared food and freezing it. To reheat, remove from the bag, zap in the microwave to thaw, and then heat in the oven until hot and crisp.

I've been making this sauce for some time now and friends and family have been asking me to make it for them and then telling me I should sell it at markets! I love this sauce and put it on anything, from my gourmet sausage rolls (page 80), lamb and rosemary pies (page 77), fried eggs on toast in the morning, sausage and tomato sandwiches ... you get the point, I love this sauce and I'm sure you will, too. It does have a little bit of a bite to it so you can adjust the heat by adding more or less of the cayenne and chipotle—I say add more!

SMOKY BARBECUE SAUCE

1 tablespoon olive oil

1 tin (400 g/14 oz) chopped tomatoes

100 g (3½ oz/½ cup lightly packed) brown sugar, plus 2 tablespoons extra

375 ml (13 fl oz/1½ cups) stout

60 ml (2 fl oz/¼ cup) apple cider vinegar

2 tablespoons worcestershire sauce

3 dried bay leaves

2 tablespoons salt

2 tablespoons garlic powder

2 tablespoons onion powder

2 tablespoons smoked paprika

1 tablespoon celery seeds

1 tablespoon freshly ground black pepper

1 tablespoon chilli powder

1 tablespoon cayenne pepper

1 tablespoon chipotle flakes, ground to a powder

Heat the olive oil in a saucepan over medium–high heat, then add the tomatoes and cook for several minutes, stirring frequently. Add the sugar, stout, vinegar and worcestershire sauce, and stir to combine. Bring to the boil, then reduce the heat and simmer for 10 minutes.

Finely chop the bay leaves and put into a spice blender or hand-held blender bowl. Add the salt and pulse the blender to break down the bay leaves further. Add the garlic powder and pulse until the bay leaves are finely crumbled. Add the remaining ingredients and blend to combine.

Add 2 tablespoons of the dry spice mix to the simmering sauce (or 3 if you want it hot and 4 if you want it really hot) and stir through well. Continue to simmer for another 20 minutes to extract and combine the flavours from the spice mix into the sauce. Transfer the hot sauce into a blender and blend until smooth, then return the sauce to the pan and simmer for another 10 minutes.

The sauce should be a thick pouring consistency. If you over-reduce it, add some more stout to loosen it up.

Makes about 1 litre (35 fl oz/4 cups)

When I think of salad I don't think of coleslaw, I think of green leaves and tomatoes. In my mind, coleslaw has outgrown its salad label and become a famous and substantial dish in its own right. So famous, in fact, that it is no longer known by its old moniker and is instantly recognisable by the mouth-watering title of 'slaw! 'Slaw is simple, uncomplicated, incredibly moreish and a great accompaniment to almost anything.

'SLAW

75 g (2⅔ oz/1 cup) thinly sliced green cabbage

75 g (2⅔ oz/1 cup) thinly sliced red cabbage

50 g (1¾ oz/½ cup) thinly sliced snow peas (mangetout)

1 carrot, julienned

2 cheeks red capsicum (pepper), thinly sliced

2 tablespoons mixed seeds (pepitas/pumpkin seeds, sunflower and pine nuts)*

Dressing

235 g (8½ oz/1 cup) whole-egg mayonnaise

55 g (2 oz/¼ cup) caster (superfine) sugar

2 tablespoons white wine vinegar

2 teaspoons horseradish cream

salt and freshly ground black pepper

Put all the 'slaw ingredients in a large salad bowl and mix to combine well.

To make the dressing, put all the ingredients in a small bowl, taste for seasoning and whisk to combine well. Pour the dressing over the 'slaw, toss together and serve.

Feeds 2–4

NOTE

You can find mixed seeds in health food shops or the health food aisle of your supermarket.

Making bread is one of those things we all seem to have a go at and then lose interest in. I mean, why make your own bread when there are so many good bakeries out there that can make it for you? Well, because making bread is fun, it's great to make with the kids and you get to make recipes like this one. You can make a basic bread dough or a fancy one with speciality flours like spelt, it's up to you.

MY ITALIAN BREAD

Basic Dough
3 teaspoons dried yeast
1 teaspoon olive oil, plus extra to grease the bowl
½ teaspoon sugar
600 g (1 lb 5 oz/4 cups) strong flour
1 teaspoon salt

Italian Flavours
45 g (1⅔ oz/¼ cup) kalamata olives
55 g (2 oz/¼ cup) semi-dried tomatoes
2 rosemary sprigs
35 g (1¼ oz) small diced pecorino cheese
55 g (2 oz) thinly sliced salami (optional)

Put the yeast, olive oil and sugar in a mixing bowl with 350 ml (12 fl oz) of warm water, and give it a good stir so the sugar dissolves and the oil mixes through. Set aside for about 15 minutes while the yeast activates and begins to froth up.

Put the flour in the bowl of an electric mixer, if you have one, and add the salt and mix through. Attach the dough hook, turn on the mixer and slowly add the yeast mixture. Keep mixing until the dough forms a ball then turn the dough out onto a floured work surface and knead for about 10 minutes.

If you don't have an electric mixer, mix the flour and salt together on your floured work surface, make a well in the middle and slowly use your hands to mix in some of the yeast mixture. Continue this process, incorporating the yeast mixture into the flour, until all the mixture is combined and you have a ball of dough. You may need to use some extra liquid, in which case add a little more warm water from the tap. If you use too much liquid and the dough is very sticky, then sprinkle in some extra flour.

Impress your friends and their tastebuds by making something really delicious and truly unique next time the footy's on ... Even better, get them into the kitchen to help out.

Once kneaded thoroughly, lightly oil a bowl and sprinkle some flour in the bottom and around the sides to lightly coat. Put the dough in the bowl, cover with a tea towel (dish towel) or plastic wrap and leave to rest until it has doubled in size.

Meanwhile, cut the flesh from the olives and remove the pips, and chop the semi-dried tomatoes—think rustic! Chop the rosemary—I use about 2 teaspoons.

Remove the dough from the bowl and place on the floured work surface. Knock it back and then flatten it out a little. Put all the Italian ingredients on the flattened dough and then knead well to mix the olives, tomatoes, cheese, salami, if using, and rosemary through. Shape the dough to your liking (or put into an oiled baking tin), place the dough onto a lightly oiled baking tray and leave to double in size again.

Preheat the oven to 200°C (400°F) (fan-forced 180°C/350°F).

Place the Italian dough in the oven and cook for about 35–45 minutes. You can tell it is cooked by flicking the bottom of the loaf with your finger, if it sounds hollow it is cooked.

To serve, cut and eat! You don't really need anything else with this as the bread has plenty of flavour! If anything have a glass of Chianti. Ciao!

Yes, you need an ice-cream maker to make this dish but they are fairly inexpensive and once you start to make your own ice cream you will wonder why you haven't until now. The trick with this ice cream is to serve it up without telling people it has chilli in it and then watch the looks on their faces as the cold ice cream begins to heat up in their mouth! Actually, that would be cruel, especially if you have used a really hot variety of chilli!

CHOCOLATE CHILLI ICE CREAM

125 ml (4 fl oz/½ cup) milk
160 g (5¾ oz) caster (superfine) sugar
1 free-range egg, beaten
500 ml (17 fl oz/2 cups) pouring cream

1 fatalii chilli or habanero chilli, halved*
100 g (3½ oz) dark chocolate (70% cocoa), grated

Put all the ingredients except the chocolate in a saucepan and heat gently until all the sugar is dissolved. Stir well so the egg is well combined. When the mixture is quite warm—do not boil or simmer—add the chocolate and stir through to melt. (There will still be some grainy little specks of chocolate floating in the mixture, which is fine.) Make sure you keep tasting the mixture as it is cooking to judge how much heat you get from the chilli. When you think it is hot enough remove the chilli and discard. If you are really brave you can finely chop the chilli before adding it to the mix and then leave it in the finished product. Once melted, pour the mixture into a container and chill in the fridge or freezer.

Put the chilled mixture into the ice-cream machine and churn, following the manufacturer's instructions, to achieve the desired consistency.

Makes around 1 litre (35 fl oz/4 cups)

NOTE

You can use any hot chilli you want from small red Thai chillies or bird's-eye chillies, to jalapeños to the very hot habaneros. I like to use fataliis which have a rich fruity, almost mango-like, aroma and flavour and they are also very hot! They can be difficult to find, which is why I suggest using a habanero. You can also use whatever chocolate you desire—dairy milk will give a more creamy chocolate character than, say, a rich dark chocolate, and if you feel adventurous you could use 125 ml (4 fl oz/½ cup) of stout in place of the milk.

The following recipe is enough for four beautiful slightly dense, delightfully textured, wonderfully sweet with a hint of spice, cakes. I originally developed this recipe for just two cakes, but to be perfectly honest, you may as well double this recipe—that way you can share them with your family and friends. They really are that delicious!

ORANGE DRIZZLE CAKES

100 g (3½ oz) unsalted butter, softened
250 g (9 oz) caster (superfine) sugar
4 drops natural vanilla extract
2 free-range eggs
2 teaspoon grated orange zest
80 g (2¾ oz) self-raising flour

40 g (1½ oz) almond meal
2 tablespoons milk
170 ml (5½ fl oz/⅔ cup) orange juice
4 pieces orange rind
4 slices orange, no skin or pith
8 cardamom pods, slightly crushed

Preheat the oven to 180°C (350°F) (fan-forced 160°C/315°F).

Put 100 g (3½ oz) of the caster sugar and the butter in the bowl of an electric mixer and beat until creamed and well combined. While the beater is still beating, add the vanilla extract and the eggs and beat until combined. Add the orange zest and beat until combined. Stop the beaters, add the flour and almond meal, then put the beater back down and gently combine well. Add the milk and mix well.

Take four ramekins (about 8.5 cm/3½ in diametre by 7 cm/2¾ in deep) or you could use a muffin tray or even a cup cake tray, and butter the insides and bottoms. Cut out four discs of baking paper that will fit snugly in the bottom of each ramekin and butter the top of the paper once it is in the ramekin. Divide the mixture equally between the four ramekins and place on an oven rack in the middle of the oven. Cook for about 25 minutes or until a skewer stuck into the centre of a cake comes out clean.

Meanwhile, put a small saucepan over medium heat. Add the orange juice and the remaining 150 g (5½ oz/⅔ cup) of caster sugar and bring to the boil, stirring so the sugar dissolves. Reduce the heat to a gentle simmer and add the orange rind, orange slices and the cardamom pods and simmer for 10 minutes, stirring occasionally. Remove from the heat.

Remove the cakes from the oven and run a knife around the side of each ramekin, then put a plate over the top, one at a time, and tip the whole lot over so the ramekin is sitting upside down on the plate. Carefully lift the ramekin, leaving the cake behind. Turn the cake back over and use the skewer to gently stab down into the cake from top to bottom, 15 or so times—this will allow the syrup to run into the cake. Repeat with the remaining cakes.

To serve, place the cakes on separate plates, discard the cardamom pods and spoon the syrup over the top of the cakes, drenching them well. Drape a slice of orange over the top, spoon over some more syrup and put a piece of rind on each cake. Serve with a dollop of cream or a scoop of good vanilla ice cream.

Serves 4

>>>>>>>>>>>>>>>>>>>>>>>>
TIP
You can make the cakes and syrup ahead of time—when it comes time to serve, zap the cakes in the microwave for about 30–45 seconds so they are hot and place on serving plates. Reheat the syrup on the stove and pour over.
>>>>>>>>>>>>>>>>>>>>>>>>

CHAPTER 3

Eat your VEGGIES!

I was going to call this chapter KISS, as in Keep it Superbly Simple or Keep it Sensationally Simple or Keep it Stunningly Simple or even Keep it Simply Simple, instead I called it, as you may have already noticed, Eat Your Veggies! Why you ask? Well, what can be simpler than the humble vegetable? There is something so nourishing and comforting about them, you can almost feel your body smile in satisfaction as you indulge in a big bowl of soup or salad or risotto made with only a few wonderfully simple ingredients. There is a place for complicated big-flavoured dishes that smack you about the head when you eat them and, indeed, there are plenty of those recipes in the other chapters, but life is about balance. Sometimes, all I want is a simple plate of slightly burnt beans or a soul-warming soup or a wonderfully light salad that just sings healthy tunes. By making sure we eat our veggies we can maintain balance, harmony and health in the kitchen, on our plates, in our bowls and in our bodies.

I'm not sure how I came up with this dish, but most likely I was cooking a stir-fry in my wok and added the beans when it was smoking, and in an attempt not to burn them outright I tossed them around, quickly added some garlic, salt and (knowing me) some chilli and then pulled them out of the wok, blackened in places but perfectly cooked and seasoned! The dish has changed a bit since then, but from that day on burnt beans became a favourite dish of mine. These are great as a snack with a beer or they make a terrific side to pretty much anything—try them with the Argentine empanadas on page 60, the beer-marinated barbecued veal rib-eye on page 141 or the beer and herb–marinated barbecued chicken on page 142.

JUST A LITTLE BIT BURNT BEANS

2 tablespoons olive oil
250 g (9 oz) green beans, top and tailed
3 garlic cloves, crushed

pinch of salt
1 heaped tablespoon slivered almonds

Put a good heavy-based frying pan over high heat and let it get really hot. Tip in the olive oil and, when it is smoking a little, add the beans. Give the pan a bit of a shake to move the beans around and a bit of a toss to turn them over—you want to get some colour all over, if you let the beans sit they will burn too much and only on one side. Once you start to see the beans beginning to char in places—after about 2 minutes—add the garlic and, if need be, a little more oil and give everything a good toss. Once well combined and the beans have a few little char or burn marks on them, season with some salt, add the almonds and give everything a final toss to combine.

   Remove from the heat and serve.

Feeds 4

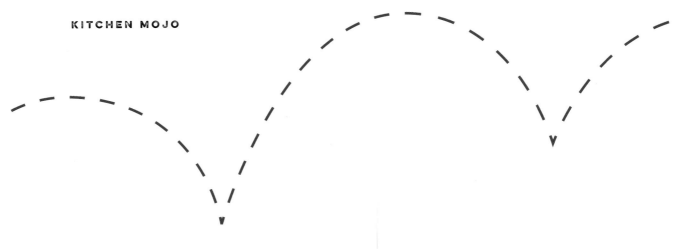

You can't get a more simple salad than this, so it's all about the ingredients and the dressing. Salad dressings can be super simple or you can get a little more complicated if you want. The main thing is that no matter how easy grabbing a bottle of dressing mix at the supermarket can be, making your own is even easier and will always taste better and be better for you, too! The most important thing is to use a great quality olive oil and a really good balsamic vinegar and build from there. The tomatoes are optional as the salad is really soft without them and not quite as soft with them in, thanks to their acidity—your choice.

SOFT SALAD

1 butter lettuce
1 large Lebanese (short) cucumber, peeled, halved
    lengthways and sliced
1 avocado, diced
1 punnet (250 g/9 oz) cherry tomatoes (optional),
    halved or quartered if large

2 tablespoons olive oil
2 tablespoons balsamic vinegar
salt and freshly ground black pepper

Pull the lettuce apart, put it in a salad spinner, give it a good wash then spin it dry. Put the lettuce in a salad bowl, add the cucumber, avocado and tomatoes, if using, and give it all a toss. Combine the olive oil and vinegar in a jar and give it a shake to combine, season with salt and pepper and shake again. Taste for seasoning and balance, and then pour it over the salad. Toss the salad again and serve.

    This is a great side salad that you could serve with any grilled meat (chops, chicken, snags or fish), but I often have this salad just as it is for lunch!

Feeds 4

This is one of my 'go to' salads whenever we have people over for a barbecue. It is deceptively simple in as much as it looks pretty modest, but the flavours are terrific—the textures in the salad combine really well and the sweet and sour in the dressing brings it all together. We would normally serve this with a warm potato salad (page 102) and soft salad (page 96) and lots of snags on the barbie. That said, it is great on its own as a lunch salad or a light healthy dinner.

RICE SALAD

330 g (11⅔ oz/1½ cups) medium-grain brown rice
1 red capsicum (pepper)
1 yellow capsicum (pepper)
1 large zucchini (courgette)
4 spring onions (scallions)
1 tin (420 g/15 oz) corn kernels
40 g (1½ oz) sultanas (golden raisins)
2 tablespoons sunflower seeds

Dressing
juice of ½ lemon (about 1 tablespoon)
60 ml (2 fl oz/¼ cup) olive oil
2 teaspoons honey
1 teaspoon wholegrain mustard
salt and freshly ground black pepper

Cook the rice, following the packet instructions, then set aside to cool slightly.

Finely dice the capsicum and the zucchini and put in a large salad bowl. Thinly slice the spring onions and add to the bowl. Drain the tin of corn and add to the bowl along with the sultanas and sunflower seeds. Add the warm rice and give everything a really good mix.

For the dressing, combine the lemon juice, olive oil, honey and mustard in a jar. Season with salt and pepper, put the lid on and give it a good shake. Taste and adjust the flavours as needed. Pour over the salad and mix through.

Feeds 6 as a main or 10 as a side

I call this my super food salad because every ingredient in this recipe is classed in one way or another as a super food—even the dressing ingredients. Edamame are young soya beans still in the pod—you can buy these from specialist Asian food stores and major supermarkets in the freezer section. They make for a delicious snack—just put them in a bowl and steam or microwave them until hot, then pour over some soy sauce and sprinkle with salt, and suck the beans out of the pod—perfect with a beer which, sadly, is not a super food.

SUPER FOOD SALAD WITH AVOCADO DRESSING

110 g (3¾ oz/½ cup) brown, green or puy lentils (don't use red lentils as they turn to mush when cooked)

6–8 baby beetroot (beets) (or 2–3 large ones or tinned), quartered*

150 g (5½ oz/2 cups) very finely shredded Tuscan kale (don't use the centre stem—cut it out and discard)

20 g (1 oz/½ cup) edamame beans (or more if you like), squeezed out of the pods

8 cherry tomatoes, quartered

½ red onion, thinly sliced

1 small carrot, julienned

3 tablespoons pepitas (pumpkin seeds)

large pinch of dill

¼ teaspoon honey

Avocado Dressing

1 tablespoon mashed avocado

1 tablespoon Greek-style yoghurt

1 teaspoon lemon juice

1 teaspoon olive oil

1 small garlic clove, crushed

salt and freshly ground black pepper

Put the lentils in a saucepan and cover with 250 ml (9 fl oz/1 cup) of cold water. (Don't salt the water as that can make the lentils tough.) Place the pan over high heat and bring to the boil, then reduce the heat and simmer for 15–20 minutes or until the lentils are *al dente*. Strain and set aside.

If you are using fresh baby beetroot, scrub clean, top and tail, then place in a small saucepan, cover with cold water and add a little salt. Bring to the boil then reduce the heat and simmer until the beetroot are tender all the way through. Drain and when cool enough to handle peel and cut into quarters. If you have used larger beetroots then cut those into eighths.

To make the dressing, combine the avocado, yoghurt, lemon juice, olive oil and garlic in a small bowl and whisk to combine. Season with salt and pepper and whisk again, then taste for seasoning and adjust as needed.

Combine all the salad ingredients, in a large bowl then pour in the dressing and give the salad a really good stir to evenly combine.

Feeds 4 as an entrée or 2 as a main

NOTE

I love this salad as it is, but being a meat eater I just can't help adding some hot smoked ocean trout to it when the mood strikes me. Use a mixture of red and golden beetroot for added colour.

This is one of those salads that I'm happy to eat on its own for lunch or to serve up as a perfect accompaniment to whatever else I have cooked—be it a steak, barbecued quail or some roast chicken. My favourite dish to serve this with, though, is my tea-smoked brined eye fillet on page 137—it's a fantastic combination, and great for a dinner party.

LENTIL, PARSLEY AND TOMATO SALAD

325 g (11½ oz/1½ cups) brown lentils
1 garlic clove, smashed
2 bay leaves
12 large cherry tomatoes, halved
   then some cut into three
½ red onion, thinly sliced
2 Lebanese (short) cucumbers, cut into large dice
1 tablespoon small capers
1 bunch flat–leaf (Italian) parsley, leaves only
12 caperberries (optional)

Dressing
100 ml (3½ fl oz) olive oil
80 ml (2½ fl oz/⅓ cup) balsamic vinegar
1 tablespoon lemon juice
1 tablespoon red wine vinegar
1 garlic clove, crushed
1 teaspoon wholegrain mustard
salt and freshly ground black pepper

Put the lentils, smashed garlic and bay leaves in a large saucepan with 1.5 litres (52 fl oz/6 cups) of cold water. Place the pan over high heat and bring to the boil, then reduce the heat and simmer for 15–20 minutes or until the lentils are *al dente*. Strain, remove and discard the garlic and bay leaves and set the lentils aside to cool.

For the dressing, put the olive oil, balsamic, lemon juice, red wine vinegar, crushed garlic, mustard, salt and pepper into a jar and shake well to combine— taste for seasoning and adjust as needed.

Combine the rest of the salad ingredients in a bowl. Add the warm lentils, then give it another mix to combine. Pour over the dressing and mix again to combine well.

Feeds 6 as a main or 10 as a side

This is a very basic but very delicious potato salad that goes brilliantly with anything barbecued. You can add other ingredients such as capers, gherkins, prosciutto, hard-boiled eggs, smoked fish, sour cream, dill or chives—which are all fantastic—however, this is a simple salad we make at home all the time. Oh, I should also confess that this is not my recipe, but my mother-in-law's.

WARM POTATO SALAD

1 kg (2 lb 4 oz) baby potatoes (sometimes known
   as cocktail potatoes)
salt
2 teaspoons olive oil
5 short-cut bacon rashers, rind removed, diced
   (optional)

235 g (8½ oz/1 cup) whole-egg mayonnaise
60 ml (2 fl oz/¼ cup) pouring cream
freshly ground black pepper
4 spring onions (scallions), thinly sliced

Put the potatoes with their skins still on in a large saucepan, fill with plenty of cold water, add ¼ teaspoon of salt and then bring to the boil over high heat. Reduce the heat to what I like to call an excited simmer and cook until the potatoes are cooked—be careful not to overcook or you will end up with a mushy salad. The potatoes are cooked when you can insert a fork or knife into the centre of them without feeling any firmness or resistance. Tip the potatoes into a colander to drain and leave to cool just enough so you can handle them—but don't let them go cold—it's a warm potato salad!

Meanwhile, while the potatoes are cooking, heat the olive oil in a frying pan over medium–high heat. Add the bacon and cook gently for about 8–10 minutes, stirring frequently, until cooked and crispy, then transfer onto paper towel to drain. Combine the mayonnaise and cream and mix well, then season with salt and pepper. Cut the potatoes into quarters, place in a large serving bowl, tip in the bacon, if using, and spring onions and give it all a gentle stir—the heat from the potatoes will release and combine all the yummy flavours together. Add the cream and mayonnaise mixture and gently mix through evenly.

Feeds 6–8

This dish was a bit of a crazy cheesy experiment I did in an episode of my cooking show, *Mercurio's Menu*. If you guessed the episode was all about cheese, then you guessed correctly. I actually cooked it at a food awards ceremony and as people seemed to really like it I thought I would include it here. I originally served it on a little tray of crispy oven-baked prosciutto for a bit of textural crunch, but I've left the prosciutto out here to keep things meat free!

FIG BAKED ON FETA WITH A THREE-CHEESE SAUCE

125 ml (4 fl oz/½ cup) balsamic vinegar
55 g (2 oz/¼ cup) caster (superfine) sugar
250 g (9 oz) feta cheese
2 large figs (½ each per serve)
raw sugar
12 g (¼ oz) butter
12 g (¼ oz) plain (all-purpose) flour

250–375 ml (9–13 fl oz/1–1½ cups) milk
50 g (1¾ oz) ripe brie cheese, rind removed and discarded, chopped
35 g (1¼ oz) gouda cheese, grated
35 g (1¼ oz) jarlsberg cheese, grated
freshly ground black pepper

Preheat the oven to 200°C (400°F) (fan-forced 180°C/350°F).

To make the syrup, put the vinegar and sugar in a small saucepan over high heat, stir to combine and then bring to the boil. Turn down the heat a little so that it is a rolling simmer rather than a rolling boil and reduce by about three-quarters. Set aside.

Cover the base of a baking tray with a layer of foil, then place a sheet of baking paper on top of that. Cut the feta into eight long pieces and lay two pieces side by side on top of the baking paper. Cut each fig in half from the top of the stem right down the middle and lay one half, flesh side up, on top of each feta square. Repeat until you have four squares of feta each with half a fig laying across it. Sprinkle each fig with a pinch of raw sugar. Put the tray in the oven and bake for 10 minutes.

Meanwhile, to make the cheese sauce, melt the butter in a saucepan over medium–high heat. When it foams add the flour and stir to combine. Continue to cook and stir the flour for about 5 minutes. Gradually add some milk and stir vigorously to combine—I like to use a whisk for this. Continue to add milk, a little at a time, whisking, until you get a nice smooth and creamy texture—you may not need to use all the milk. Add the brie and stir to combine, then add the gouda and the jarlsberg. Stir well to combine and season with pepper. The sauce should be like a thick runny custard.

Remove the feta and figs from the oven and use an egg slide to lift them off the baking tray and place on each plate. Drizzle about 2 tablespoons of the cheese sauce over and across the fig so that it falls on the fig and down the side onto the feta cheese. Drizzle some of the balsamic syrup around the plate and serve.

Feeds 4 as an entrée

I love asparagus but had never thought of making a soup using it as the theme ingredient—in fact, I can't remember why or how I started experimenting with it, but I'm glad I did! I would normally steam, grill, barbecue or stir-fry this wonderful vegetable and add it as a side to whatever the main dish was. Asparagus is such a versatile vegetable, and when it is in season it is utterly brilliant. I love the smoky character and the sweetness the bacon and bacon bones give this soup, however, if you want a vegetarian dish, leave them out—to get the smoky character that the bacon provides you could add two or three tablespoons of smoky paprika and a tablespoon of chipotle flakes or powder instead. You can eat this soup cold—it's perfect on a hot summer's day.

ASPARAGUS SOUP

2 tablespoons olive oil
3 tablespoons unsalted butter
1 leek, white part only, halved lengthways and thinly sliced
1 red onion, roughly chopped
4 streaky bacon rashers, rind removed and discarded, cut into thin strips (optional)
2 garlic cloves, finely chopped

2 large potatoes, roughly chopped
1.2 kg (2 lb 10 oz) fresh asparagus
1.5 litres (52 fl oz/6 cups) vegetable stock
600 g (1 lb 5 oz) smoked bacon bones (optional)
½ teaspoon lemon thyme leaves
sea salt and freshly ground black pepper
150 ml (5 fl oz) pouring cream (optional)

Heat the olive oil and butter in a large flameproof casserole dish or saucepan over medium heat. Add the leek and gently sauté for 5 minutes, then add the onion and cook for about 5 minutes more. If using the bacon, stir through, and cook for 3–5 minutes—you don't want to brown the bacon, just release its flavour. (If you are going strictly vego for this soup add the smoky paprika and chipotle—see introduction—to the leek and onion and cook for a couple of minutes to allow the fragrance to come out.) Stir through the garlic and cook for several minutes. (Sometimes spice powders will absorb the oil and the pan will go dry, if this happens add a little more butter and oil before adding the potatoes.) Add the potatoes, mixing so they are well coated with the spice mix and continue to cook.

Meanwhile, prepare the asparagus. Snap the woody stems off the bottoms to yield about 800 g (1 lb 12 oz) of asparagus spears. Put the asparagus in a colander and give them a wash, then cut into 4 cm (1½ in) lengths. Add the chopped asparagus to the pan and mix everything through. Add the vegetable stock, bacon bones, if using, and the lemon thyme, season with salt and pepper, then bring to the boil. Reduce the heat and simmer, uncovered, for about 45–60 minutes.

Remove the bacon bones and discard. Use a hand-held blender to blend the soup into a smooth consistency. Check for seasoning and adjust as needed.

You can add cream when blending if you want a creamy flavour and texture or just have it as is.

Feeds 6

I first made this soup for a TV show I was shooting in Launceston which featured not just cauliflower but also some of the first truffles being harvested in Australia! With truffles fetching upwards of $2000 per kilo I thought I would leave them out of this recipe, but hey if you want to give it a go don't let me stop you. But considering a cauliflower will set you back only a few dollars at most, maybe you can stretch your budget for a truffle slice or two!?

CAULIFLOWER SOUP

1 tablespoon butter
2 tablespoons olive oil
1 celery stalk, thinly sliced
1 leek, white part only, thinly sliced
1 cauliflower head (about 600–700 g/
   1 lb 5 oz–1 lb 9 oz), chopped
250 ml (9 fl oz/1 cup) milk
750 ml (26 fl oz/3 cups) chicken or vegetable stock

¼ teaspoon nutmeg
1 bay leaf
125 ml (4 fl oz/½ cup) pouring cream
salt and freshly ground black pepper
4–6 thick slices day-old sourdough bread
35 g (1¼ oz/⅓ cup) freshly grated parmesan cheese
chilli powder (optional)

Preheat the oven to 220°C (415°F) (fan-forced 200°C/400°F).

Heat the butter and 1 tablespoon of the olive oil in a large saucepan over medium–high heat and when hot add the celery and leek and sweat down for 5 minutes. Add the cauliflower and continue to cook, stirring, for 5 minutes to caramelise the flavours. Add the milk, stock, nutmeg and bay leaf, bring to the boil and then reduce the heat to a simmer. Cook until the cauliflower is tender.

Once the cauliflower is cooked remove the bay leaf then put the soup in a blender, or use a hand-held blender, and blend until silky smooth. If using a blender return the soup to the pan, place over a gentle heat, add the cream and stir through to combine well. Continue to heat the soup until hot, and taste for seasoning.

While the soup is simmering away, remove the crusts from the bread (feed to your local ducks) then tear or pick into small pieces—you want large textured crumbs. Put the crumbs in a bowl and drizzle with the remaining oil, give it a toss to evenly coat, season with a little salt and then toss again. Tip the crumbs onto a baking tray and cook until golden and crisp. Tip the crumbs onto paper towel and then sprinkle generously with grated parmesan and a little chilli powder if you want. Shake to cover evenly and keep warm.

Serve the soup in individual bowls with a spoonful of parmesan bread crumbs in the middle as a crunchy garnish.

Feeds 6–8

This is definitely one of those dishes that is best described as a 'hug in a bowl'. It is so warming, inviting and earthy that with every spoonful you feel more and more loved and comforted. It is a dish that I have been making for years and will for years to come. It is the perfect winter soup— but a warning to veggie readers, it does contain pork hock so you might want to give it a miss.

LENTIL SOUP

1 tablespoon olive oil
1 tablespoon butter
1 brown onion, diced
2 carrots, diced
3 celery stalks, diced
2 tins (800 g/1 lb 12 oz) crushed tomatoes
2 litres (70 fl oz/8 cups) chicken stock

375 g (13 oz) green or brown lentils
2 bay leaves
1 smoked pork hock
¼ teaspoon chilli flakes (optional, if you like a little bit of heat)
¼–½ teaspoon freshly ground black pepper

Heat the olive oil and butter in a large heavy-based saucepan over medium–high heat. Add the onion and cook for several minutes, stirring. Add the carrot and celery, and cook, stirring, for about 5 minutes. Add the tomatoes, stir through and bring to the boil. Add the stock, lentils and bay leaves, stir and bring back to the boil. Add the hock and chilli flakes, if using, and give it all a really good stir. Bring to the boil, cover, reduce the heat to low and simmer gently for 1½–2 hours, turning the hock over every 30 minutes until the meat from the hock starts to pull easily away from the bone.

Remove the hock from the soup, pull all the meat from the bone, discarding the skin and any fat, and then shred or chop the meat. Put the meat back in the pan and stir through. Taste the soup for seasoning and add salt and pepper as needed—the hock has been brined prior to smoking, so that can make the meat fairly salty already, but I do add a generous amount of black pepper.

Feeds 6–8

To get an authentic smokiness for this recipe you could smoke the tomatoes over wood chips, but that takes a lot more work. Instead, I take an easier route and settle for smokiness from the smoked paprika and chipotle powder, which also combine to give a lovely depth and sweetness— and seeing that a chipotle is a dried smoked jalapeño it also gives some background heat. You could also peel the tomatoes by cutting a cross in the bottom of them and immersing them in boiling water for 30 seconds and then peeling. That said, if you have really ripe tomatoes peeling can be a little difficult which is why I don't bother.

SMOKY TOMATO SOUP

2 tablespoons olive oil
2 tablespoons unsalted butter
1 brown onion, diced
1 garlic clove, finely chopped
3 tablespoons smoked paprika
1 tablespoon chipotle powder
2 teaspoons chopped oregano
1 kg (2 lb 4 oz) ripe tomatoes, core cut out
    and roughly chopped

375 ml (13 fl oz/1½ cups) chicken or vegetable
    stock
2 dried bay leaves
salt and freshly ground black pepper
1 tablespoon pouring cream
toasted baguette with gruyere cheese, to serve
    (optional)

Heat the olive oil and butter in a flameproof casserole dish over medium–high heat, then add the onion and fry gently for about 8 minutes. Add the garlic and cook for 2 minutes, then add the paprika, chipotle and oregano and cook for a couple of minutes so the flavours can really combine. Add the tomatoes, increase the heat and bring to the boil, then give them a good stir. Add the stock and bay leaves, reduce the heat and simmer gently for about 30 minutes.

Remove the soup from the heat. Remove the bay leaves and discard. Taste the soup for seasoning, adding salt and black pepper as needed. Use a hand-held blender to blend the soup into a thick, smooth consistency. Add the cream and mix through. Return to the stovetop and heat through before serving.

Serve with slices of toasted baguette with gruyère cheese melted on top.

Feeds 4–6

This is a great soup that requires a little bit of work—roasting and peeling the chestnuts. If you don't want to make the effort though, you can also buy peeled fresh frozen chestnuts from specialist delis which will certainly cut down the preparation time. I also like to use speck in this soup as it adds a sweetness and earthiness that I like, but as this chapter has vegetables in the starring role you can leave it out.

ROASTED CHESTNUT AND WILD MUSHROOM SOUP

1 kg (2 lb 4 oz) fresh unpeeled chestnuts (or 650 g/ 1 lb 7 oz peeled fresh or frozen chestnuts)
60 ml (2 fl oz/¼ cup) olive oil
1½ tablespoons unsalted butter
1 brown onion, diced
100 g (3½ oz) speck or pancetta, diced (optional)
2 garlic cloves, finely chopped
1 chilli, thinly sliced

8 sage leaves
350 g (12 oz) saffron milk cap mushrooms, wiped clean and roughly chopped*
150 g (5½ oz) slippery jack mushrooms, wiped clean and roughly chopped
1.5 litres (52 fl oz/6 cups) chicken stock or vegetable stock
salt and freshly ground black pepper

If using fresh chestnuts, preheat the oven to 240°C (475°F) (fan-forced 220°C/415°F).

Cut a cross in the flat side of each chestnut shell—this helps the steam escape and also makes them easier to peel. Put the chestnuts on a baking tray and roast for about 20–30 minutes. Keep an eye on them—they become tough and inedible when they are overcooked. Remove from the oven, wrap in a clean tea towel (dish towel) and leave to sweat for about 15 minutes. Next comes the hardest part about using fresh chestnuts—peeling. The outer hard shell is easy to get off, but the brown skin over the flesh is harder. You should get around 650–700 g (1 lb 7 oz–1 lb 9 oz), depending on how successful you were at peeling them. If you use raw peeled chestnuts they need to be boiled for about 45 minutes first. If you use frozen chestnuts, follow the instructions on the packet.

Heat the olive oil and butter in a large saucepan over medium–high heat, then add the onion and cook for about 5 minutes. Add the speck, if using, and the garlic and chilli. Thinly slice five of the sage leaves, add to the pan and cook for another 5 minutes or so. Add the chopped mushrooms and cook them down for about 10 minutes, stirring occasionally. Add the stock and bring to a simmer, then add the chestnuts and remaining sage leaves, and stir well. Cover with a lid, reduce the heat and simmer gently for 20 minutes.

Blend the soup in a blender or use a hand-held blender, but make sure to leave some chunky bits of mushroom and chestnuts to add some texture. Return to the heat and bring to a simmer, then taste for seasoning and adjust as needed.

Serve in separate bowls with some buttered crusty sourdough bread if you like.

Feeds 6

NOTE

Use any mushroom combination you want. Your local market should provide some exotic combinations— just make sure you get 500 g (1 lb 2 oz).

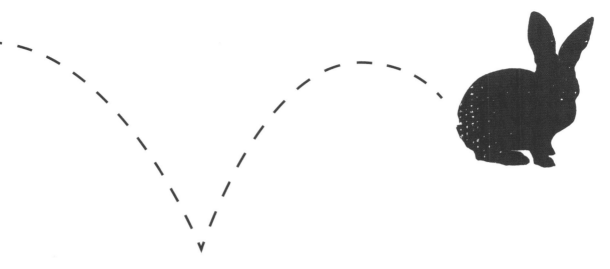

I love this recipe—it's delicious, simple, easy to make and it goes so well with so many other things. You can serve it on its own or with the salt, sugar and honey–cured salmon with wasabi mayo on page 184 or the crumbed pork chop on page 37, but I also love it with pan-fried duck and some potato roasties on the side!

BOK CHOY STIR-FRY

1 tablespoon olive oil
1 garlic clove, finely chopped
1 teaspoon finely chopped ginger
1 red bird's-eye chilli, finely chopped (optional)
300 g (10½ oz) firm tofu, cut into 2 cm (¾ in) cubes
150 g (5½ oz) oyster mushrooms, thinly sliced

2 bunches bok choy (pak choy)*
150 g (5½ oz) sugarsnap peas
1½ tablespoons soy sauce
1½ tablespoons oyster sauce
40 g (1½ oz/¼ cup) cashew nuts

Heat the olive oil in a wok. Add the garlic, ginger and chilli, if using, and stir-fry for 2 minutes. Add the tofu and mushrooms and cook for a few minutes more.

Cut the bottoms off the bok choy so you can separate the leaves, wash well under running water, then shake off the excess water. Add to the wok, along with the sugarsnap peas, stirring to coat, and cook for 3 minutes. Add the soy sauce, oyster sauce, cashews and 1 teaspoon of water, stir again, then cover with a lid and cook for 3–4 minutes until the bok choy is tender.

To serve, put equal amounts of steamed rice in four bowls and divide the bok choy stir-fry equally between the bowls, pouring over all of the sauce as well.

Feeds 4

NOTE

It may look like a lot of bok choy when you prepare it, but it really shrinks down as it cooks.

Rice is easy to make, and to make it even easier I suggest buying a rice cooker—they take the guesswork out of cooking rice. They will cook half a cup or up to five cups at a time—although you will never need to cook that much! I have been using a rice cooker for years, ever since my kids were tots (my eldest is in her mid-twenties, so I do mean years). Funnily enough though, it was only a couple of years ago that I started to flavour my rice in the rice cooker ... I don't know why it took me so long! You can make savoury rice dishes or wonderfully sweet dessert rice dishes, all it takes is a rice cooker and a little bit of imagination.

ORANGE RICE

1 tablespoon olive oil
1 small onion, diced
3 garlic cloves, crushed
2 dried bay leaves
freshly ground black pepper
150 g (5½ oz/¾ cup) basmati rice

150 g (5½ oz/¾ cup) jasmine rice
375 ml (13 fl oz/1½ cups) orange juice
185 ml (6 fl oz/¾ cup) coconut milk
1 piece orange rind (about 5 x 1 cm/2 x ½ in)
salt

Heat the olive oil in a frying pan over high heat, then add the onion and sweat down for a couple of minutes. Reduce the heat and add the garlic and bay leaves, and season with black pepper. Continue to cook gently until the onion has caramelised. Remove from the heat.

Put the rice in your rice cooker bowl and rinse with cold water three times, draining well. Add the orange juice, coconut milk, orange rind and the cooked onion, garlic and bay leaf mixture. Stir to combine, season with a little salt and black pepper, put the lid on the rice cooker and press the cook button.

Fluff up the cooked rice with a spoon, discard the bay leaves and orange rind, and serve in a large bowl. I originally made this rice to accompany my really crispy-skinned pork belly on page 140, but it will go with anything or just eat it on its own.

Feeds 6

Three of my favourite ingredients, all in the one simple delicious dish! Just a suggestion—don't use grey pumpkin for this recipe as I think it is a very bland and tasteless pumpkin. My favourite is Jap pumpkin, also known as Kent—it has a wonderful aroma and a rich full flavour—and butternut is great too.

PUMPKIN, ASPARAGUS AND FETA RISOTTO

500 g (1 lb 2 oz) pumpkin (winter squash) (either Jap or butternut), cut into 5 mm (¼ in) dice
80 ml (2½ fl oz/⅓ cup) olive oil
salt and freshly ground black pepper
1.5 litres (52 fl oz/6 cups) chicken or vegetable stock
2 tablespoons unsalted butter
1 small leek, white part only, thinly sliced

300 g (10½ oz) arborio rice
185 ml (6 fl oz/¾ cup) dry white wine (I use chardonnay)
2 bunches asparagus, woody ends trimmed and sliced on the diagonal into 2 cm (¾ in) lengths
70 g (2½ oz/½ cup) diced Greek feta cheese
1 tablespoon freshly grated parmesan cheese

Preheat the oven to 180°C (350°F) (fan-forced 160°C/315°F).

Put half of the diced pumpkin in a bowl, drizzle with enough olive oil to coat—about 2 tablespoons—toss and then season with a pinch of salt and some pepper. Tip out onto a baking tray and roast for about 10 minutes or until slightly charred and caramelised. Remove from the oven and set aside.

Put the stock in a saucepan and bring to a very gentle simmer.

Heat the remaining oil and half the butter in a separate saucepan over medium–high heat. Add the leek and cook gently, stirring occasionally, for about 5 minutes until it becomes soft and starts to smell sweet. Add the rice and the remaining pumpkin, mixing through well so that the rice and pumpkin are well coated. Cook and stir for several minutes to toast the rice and caramelise the pumpkin—it won't change colour, but it will build in flavour. Add the wine, stirring well, and allow the rice to absorb it, then add your first ladleful of stock. This is where heat management comes into play—you don't want the heat too high as it ➤➤➤

There is a place for complicated big-flavoured dishes that smack you about the head, but life is about balance. By eating our veggies we can maintain harmony and health in our bodies.

will make the rice absorb the liquid too quickly, and you don't want it too low as it will not absorb properly. For the next 30 minutes, continue to stir the rice, adding a ladleful of stock as the last one is absorbed—every 5–8 minutes or so. After you have added a fourth ladleful of stock add the asparagus and stir it through. Continue the stirring and adding process. When you add the seventh ladleful of stock, taste the rice to see if it is done—if it is still a little crunchy in the middle add an eighth ladleful of stock. Add the feta and stir through until the stock has been absorbed. Check the consistency—the rice should be *al dente*. Taste for seasoning and add salt and pepper as needed. Remove the pan from the heat and stir through the parmesan cheese and the remaining butter, making sure to combine well. Finally, add the reserved roasted pumpkin and fold through.

By the time the risotto is ready the pumpkin you cooked in the risotto should have disintegrated and become part of the sauce, adding to the rich creamy character of the risotto. Adding the roasted pumpkin at the end adds a lovely caramel/roasted character and also a textural difference.

Feeds 4

I made this terrine as part of my TV show, *Mercurio's Menu*, with produce that was growing in the veggie patch at a beef farmer's house. This is what I love about cooking and also about this recipe—just using beautiful fresh ingredients straight from the garden, whatever is in the garden, and onto the plate! There are plenty of other vegetables you could use or add to this terrine, such as grilled asparagus or artichoke, grilled baby leeks, sun-dried tomatoes, olives, mushrooms ... the list is endless. You could also add some crumbled feta cheese through one level or some goat's cheese. Make this one first and then get creative!

VEGETABLE TERRINE

4 garlic cloves, crushed

185 ml (6 fl oz/¾ cup) olive oil

3 large red capsicums (peppers) (or you could use a combination of red and yellow capsicums)

2 large eggplants (aubergines), sliced lengthways into 3 mm (⅛ in) strips

3 large zucchini (courgettes), top and tailed and sliced lengthways into 3 mm (⅛ in) strips

6 heirloom carrots (orange and yellow), sliced lengthways into 3 mm (⅛ in) strips

6 radishes, sliced lengthways into 3 mm (⅛ in) strips

1 bunch basil

1 tablespoon balsamic vinegar

salt and freshly ground black pepper

Pesto*

60 g (2¼ oz/1 cup) tightly packed basil leaves

1–2 garlic cloves (depending on how garlicky you like it)

55 g (2 oz/⅓ cup) salted macadamia nuts

30 g (1 oz/½ cup) freshly grated parmesan or provolone cheese

salt and freshly ground black pepper

Put the crushed garlic in a small bowl, add the olive oil, stir, then set aside for 15 minutes to infuse.

Preheat the barbecue hotplate to medium–high.

Spray or wipe a 22 x 12 cm (8½ x 4½ in) terrine dish or loaf (bar) tin with a little olive oil and then line the bottom and sides with a large piece of plastic wrap—it should hang over the sides.

Slice the sides off the capsicums, place on the barbecue, skin side down, and cook until the skin is blackened and blistered. Put the capsicums in a bowl and cover with plastic wrap (or place in a plastic bag) for 5 minutes—this will make the skins easier to peel off. Peel the skins off and discard. Reserve the barbecued capsicum pieces.

Brush the remaining vegetables with a little of the infused olive oil and then place, brushed side down on the barbecue hotplate. Cook the vegetables, turning and brushing with more garlic–olive oil until the veggies are cooked. Be careful not to overcook the eggplant as it can become crisp—you want it to be nicely cooked but still pliable as you will use it as the outside of the terrine and will need to fold it over the top. ➡➡

>>>>>>>>>>>>>>>>>>>>>>>
TIP
Instead of making your own pesto you could use 1 jar of good quality store-bought pesto.
>>>>>>>>>>>>>>>>>>>>>>>

←◄◄

To construct the terrine, lay two pieces of eggplant on the bottom of the terrine dish, covering it completely. Reserve two pieces to make a lid. Layer pieces of eggplant lengthways out from the bottom, overlapping the eggplant already in the dish, going up the side and over the side of the dish. Repeat with more of the eggplant until the terrine dish and sides are covered and it looks like the eggplant is flopping out of the dish. (When you fill the dish with the other vegetables you will then fold the overhanging eggplant back over the filling.)

Place a layering of each of the remaining vegetables in the terrine dish, starting with the zucchini, then the capsicum, the carrot, the radishes, then a layer of basil leaves and lastly sprinkle a little of the balsamic over the top. Then reverse the order, so a basil layer then a layer of radish, then carrot, then capsicum, then zucchini and again a little sprinkle of balsamic. Place two pieces of eggplant on top of the zucchini and fold over the hanging eggplant sides to cover the top layer of zucchini. The terrine should fill about three-quarters of the terrine dish at most. Fold over the hanging plastic to seal. Next, get a sheet of plywood or stiff cardboard that will fit inside the terrine dish and sit it over the veggies, then place something heavy on top—such as a couple of tins of tomatoes—and put the whole thing in the fridge for 3–4 hours or, even better, overnight. This will compress the terrine and set it so that when you cut it, it will hold together.

Next, make the pesto. Put all the ingredients except the olive oil in a food processor and give it a good blend, then, with the motor running, gradually add the olive oil. Once you have added half the oil, stop and scrape down the side, then turn the motor back on and continue to add the remaining olive oil. Taste for seasoning, add salt and pepper as needed, then tip into a jar and keep sealed in the fridge.

Remove the terrine from the fridge, remove the weights and unfold the plastic wrap. Holding the terrine in one hand, put a cutting board against the top of the terrine and carefully and quickly flip the terrine and cutting board over so the terrine is sitting on top of the board. Place the board on your work surface and carefully lift the terrine dish up leaving the actual vegetable terrine sitting on the board. Remove the plastic wrap and cut the terrine into 2–3 cm (¾–1¼ in) pieces— you should get eight pieces in total.

Serve one slice on each plate with a dollop of the pesto as an entrée or serve two slices per plate with additional pesto as a main. You can also add the smoky spiced haloumi from page 55 if you want to beef up this dish.

Serves 8 as an entrée or 4 as a main

I really like the idea of making these blintz as they really belong to an era that seems to have long gone. Yes, these are just thin pancakes with some fruit, but the fact they belong to my grandmother's era or your grandmother's era make them more than that.

SWEET CHEESE BLINTZ WITH BARBECUED FRUIT

1 orange, peeled
1 mandarin, peeled
60 ml (2 fl oz/¼ cup) port
125 ml (4 fl oz/½ cup) orange juice
2 tablespoons brown sugar

Crêpe
75 g (2⅔ oz/½ cup) plain (all-purpose) flour
1 teaspoon caster (superfine) sugar
130 ml (4½ fl oz) milk

1 free-range egg
pinch of salt
butter, for frying

Filling
50 g (1¾ oz) cream cheese, at room temperature
90 g (3¼ oz) cottage cheese
1 free-range egg yolk
1 tablespoon caster (superfine) sugar
grated zest of orange, mandarin and lemon

Zest the fruit and reserve the zest for the cheese filling. Cut the mandarin and orange each into four thick discs. Heat the port, juice and sugar in a saucepan over medium–high heat and stir until the sugar is dissolved. Remove from the heat, place the sliced fruit in the pan and leave to stand for a couple of hours.

Sift the flour and sugar together into a large mixing bowl. Whisk the egg and milk together and add the salt. Gradually add the milk mixture into the flour, whisking, until the pancake mixture is nice and smooth.

Chop the cream cheese into small pieces and add to a large mixing bowl. Add all the other filling ingredients and whisk until the mixture is well combined.

Preheat the oven to 180°C (350°F) (fan-forced 160°C/315°F). Preheat the barbecue to medium–high. Melt ½ teaspoon of butter in a large frying pan over medium heat. Add a quarter of the crêpe mix and swirl to cover the base. Cook until you see bubbles form on the top of the crêpe, then gently turn over and cook the other side for a minute or two. Remove the crêpe from the frying pan and set aside on a plate. Repeat to make four crêpes.

Lay one crêpe out on a cutting board and spoon two tablespoons of the cheese mix onto the middle, fold into a square, place on a baking tray fold side down, and then repeat with the other crêpes. Brush the tops with a little melted butter and put in the oven for 15 minutes. Meanwhile, remove the orange and mandarin pieces from the port mix and grill on the barbecue until lightly caramelised on both sides. Put the saucepan with the port and juice on the stove over medium–high heat and reduce to a sticky syrup. To serve, place a blintz, folded-side down on a plate, dress with the fruit and drizzle with syrup. Serve with ice cream or yoghurt.

Feeds 4

What is not to like about this elegant and simple dessert? You could use any summer fruit for this—cherries, nectarines, mangoes just to name a few—or even a combination. In winter, you could make this recipe with fresh rhubarb or lovely winter pears.

RASPBERRY MILLE FEUILLE

8 sheets filo pastry
120 g (4¼ oz) butter, melted
icing (confectioners') sugar, for dusting
450 g (1 lb) fresh raspberries
60 g (2¼ oz) caster (superfine) sugar

1 tablespoon port
2 teaspoons brown sugar
300 g (10½ oz) crème fraîche
good quality dark chocolate (70% cocoa)

Preheat the oven to 200°C (400°F) (fan-forced 180°C/350°F).

Lay a sheet of baking paper on your work surface and then lay 1 filo sheet on top of it. Brush the filo sheet with melted butter and sprinkle with some of the icing sugar. Lay another sheet over the first and repeat with the butter and icing sugar. Continue with the remaining sheets, but do not butter the final (eighth) sheet. Trim the pastry to even the edges, then cut from top to bottom into three long strips in even widths. Now make three cuts, widthways, so you end up with four equal rectangles per slice—in total you will end up with twelve separate pieces. Place the filo pieces onto a baking tray lined with baking paper and cover the top with baking paper as well. Place another tray on top—to stop the filo from rising—and bake for 15 minutes or so until golden and crispy. Keep an eye on them as they burn easily. Transfer to a wire rack to cool. (These can be stored for 1–2 days in an airtight container.)

Put 250 g (9 oz) of the raspberries in a saucepan over medium heat, add the caster sugar and gently heat, mixing well to dissolve the sugar. Reduce the heat to a simmer and cook down for 10 minutes. Remove from the heat.

Combine the port, brown sugar and crème fraîche in a bowl, taste and adjust—by that I mean adding a little more port or a little more sugar. Add the remaining raspberries and mix through.

To assemble, place four plates on your work surface and put one biscuit on each plate. Divide half the crème fraîche mixture equally between each biscuit and spread thickly, top each with another biscuit and spread the remaining crème fraîche mixture equally between the four biscuits. Place another biscuit on top and dust with some icing sugar. Drizzle the raspberry coulis around the edge of the plates and finish off with some grated chocolate.

Feeds 4

Blokes don't
EAT QUICHE!

One of my daughters often offers to make her famous quiche for dinner to which I generally exclaim, 'Blokes don't eat quiche!' In my view a main meal isn't really a meal unless it's got meat in it as the main event too.

So what's wrong with my daughter's quiche? Absolutely nothing. It's delicious, light, full of flavour and wonderful with a salad, but it isn't meaty enough, in my opinion, to be served up for a proper meal. Yes, there's bacon in it, but we all know that bacon is really a breakfast meat not a dinner meat, so for this reason quiche is not something to serve up for dinner. You can have it for lunch if you find some left over in the fridge, but for dinner ... not in my kitchen.

And just before I go any further—bacon and egg with a pastry crust isn't a quiche anyway, it's a pie!

Most people think of cooking meat as generally using four main options—beef, lamb, chicken and pork—but there is so much more out there, meats that are unique and wonderful to use at home such as emu, kangaroo, quail, venison, duck and goat.

Did you know that goat is the most widely eaten meat in the world?

Not only do you have all these diverse meats to cook with, combined with the dizzying array of cuts, such as beef brisket, lamb ribs, pig's cheeks and more, you then add the amazing variety of style of cooking—Thai, Mexican, French, Italian and Chinese, just to name a few.

So what is suitable for dinner? What would I cook you if you came over? What do I cook for myself and my wife for a meal? Well, turn the page, dear reader, and find out, but I'm sure you already know the main ingredient that the following recipes are all built around—meat, glorious meat, in all its full-flavoured goodness.

Fattoush is a Levantine salad that uses fried stale bread as an ingredient—traditionally pitta or flatbread. Some people refer to it as a Lebanese salad, but its reach extends throughout the Middle East. It's a relatively simple salad which relies on the fresh flavours of herbs, ground sumac and lemon juice. I have added my twist using bresaola (air-dried cured beef) to give it a little more earthiness and sweetness to partner with the sourness of the lemon juice and sumac. You can leave it out if you wish to make this a vegetarian option.

BEEF BRESAOLA FATTOUSH

day-old sourdough loaf
2 tablespoons olive oil
1 garlic clove
115 g (4 oz/¾ cup) hazelnuts, roughly chopped
5 red grape or teardrop tomatoes, quartered lengthways
5 yellow grape or teardrop tomatoes, quartered lengthways
15 g (½ oz/½ cup) coriander (cilantro) leaves, chopped, plus extra to garnish
15 g (½ oz/½ cup) chopped flat-leaf (Italian) parsley
3 tablespoons baby capers, fried in a little olive oil until slightly crisp

1 yellow capsicum (pepper), roughly chopped
1 large Lebanese (short) cucumber, peeled and roughly chopped
10 cos (romaine) lettuce leaves, roughly torn
120 g (4¼ oz) very thinly sliced beef bresaola, torn into pieces*

Dressing
juice of 1 lemon (about 2 tablespoons)
60 ml (2 fl oz/¼ cup) olive oil
1 garlic clove, crushed
2 teaspoons ground sumac
salt and freshly ground black pepper

Preheat the oven to 220°C (415°F) (fan-forced 200°C/400°F).

Cut the crust off the sourdough loaf and then cut into thick slices. Using your hands, tear the slices into rough chunks about 2 cm (¾ in) square to make about 2 cups worth.

Heat the olive oil in an ovenproof frying pan over high heat. Squash the garlic clove by whacking it with the flat of your cook's knife and then add it to the pan. Let the garlic fry for 1–2 minutes to flavour the oil, then turn the heat down to medium, add the bread chunks and toss so they are coated with the flavoured oil. Once coated and the oil is sucked into the bread, discard the garlic, transfer the pan into the oven and roast until the bread is crisp and toasted. Remove and set aside.

Once you have chopped, quartered, peeled and torn all of the salad ingredients put the hazelnuts, tomatoes, coriander, parsley, fried capers, capsicum, cucumber, cos lettuces leaves, crispy bread chunks and most of the bresaola in a large bowl, and give it all a good toss.

To make the dressing, put the lemon juice, olive oil, garlic, sumac, a pinch of salt and some freshly ground black pepper in a bowl. Whisk until combined and then pour over the salad.

Toss the salad to combine then garnish with a little extra chopped coriander and the reserved bresaola.

Feeds 4–6

NOTE

You can buy bresaola at gourmet delis.

I came up with this recipe for a TV show challenge where the hosts presented me with four ingredients thirty minutes before going to air and I had to come up with a dish. My ingredients were lamb backstrap, oyster mushrooms, broccolini and a pomegranate! I had never used a pomegranate before, but I must say this salad turned out absolutely delicious.

CITRUS LAMB WITH A WARM POMEGRANATE SALAD

1 lamb backstrap (about 300 g/10½ oz)
salt and freshly ground black pepper
finely grated zest of 1 lemon
finely grated zest of 1 orange
1 tablespoon each freshly chopped basil, coriander
    (cilantro) leaves and flat-leaf (Italian) parsley
2 tablespoons olive oil
150 g (5½ oz) oyster mushrooms
1 bunch broccolini
50 g (1¾ oz/¼ cup) pomegranate seeds
2 tablespoons pomegranate juice

Dressing
60 ml (2 fl oz/¼ cup) olive oil
1½ tablespoons lemon juice
1½ tablespoons orange juice
1 teaspoon honey
1 teaspoon dijon mustard
1 tablespoon each of freshly chopped basil,
    coriander (cilantro) leaves and flat-leaf (Italian)
    parsley
salt and freshly ground black pepper

Cut the lamb backstrap into three equal length pieces and season with salt and pepper. Combine the lemon and orange zest, herbs and ½ teaspoon each of salt and pepper on a plate. Roll the backstraps over the combined zest and herbs until well coated.

Heat the olive oil in a non-stick frying pan over high heat. Add the backstrap pieces and cook for a few minutes to brown on one side. Turn the lamb over and add the mushrooms, then continue to turn the lamb until evenly cooked to medium–rare—about 5–8 minutes depending on the size. When cooked to perfection remove the backstrap pieces along with the mushrooms from the pan and put on a plate, cover and set aside.

Meanwhile, cut 1 cm (½ in) off the ends of the broccolini stalks and discard. Bring a saucepan of salted water to the boil, add the broccolini and cook for 2–3 minutes or until just tender, then drain and cut in half.

To make the dressing, combine the olive oil, juices, honey, mustard and herbs in a jar, put the lid on and shake well to combine, then season with salt and pepper to taste.

Put the pomegranate seeds in a bowl. Put the mushroom and broccolini in the bowl and dress with some of the dressing. Cut the lamb into 1 cm (½ in) slices, add to the bowl and give it a toss. Arrange the salad on a plate, pour over the pomegranate juice, and serve with the remaining dressing.

Feeds 4 as an entrée

Okay, it's not really a sandwich, but I call it a sandwich because the pork has filling. I love the way stuffing and then cooking this dish seals all of those wonderful Italian flavours within the meat. So prepare yourself for the aromas that will soon fill your kitchen, flooding your senses, igniting your passion ... okay, I may be getting a little carried away, but only a little!

PORK SANDWICH ON A CAPER SAUCE

4 pork loin steaks
4 slices jarlsberg cheese
12 sun-dried tomato pieces
12 kalamata olives, pips removed, torn apart
12 basil leaves
1 cup (150 g/5½ oz) plain (all-purpose) flour
salt and freshly ground black pepper*
2 free-range eggs, beaten
120 g (4¼ oz/2 cups) fresh breadcrumbs or panko crumbs
olive oil, for shallow-frying

Caper Sauce
½ brown onion, roughly chopped
2 garlic cloves
1 red chilli (either long or short depending on how much heat you want)
3 tablespoons capers
2–3 anchovy fillets
1 tablespoon finely chopped basil
1 tablespoon finely chopped flat-leaf (Italian) parsley
60 ml (2 fl oz/¼ cup) dry red wine
1 tin (400 g/14 oz) chopped tomatoes
salt and freshly ground black pepper
olive oil, for frying

Using a sharp knife, butterfly the pork steaks down the middle and open them out like a book. Place each steak onto a sheet of plastic wrap and place another piece of plastic wrap over the top. Using a meat mallet or a rolling pin gently beat the steaks, thinning them out and stretching them so that they become half as big again as before you started. Be careful not to make them too thin and tear holes in them and make sure you beat the spine or middle part of the steaks down flat. You can also ask your butcher to do this for you.

Remove the top layer of plastic wrap from each steak. Place a slice of cheese in the middle, then place three pieces of sun-dried tomato, the slivers from three kalamata olives and three basil leaves on top of the cheese. Now fold the right side of the steak up and over the mix, then fold the left side up and over so that it rests on top of the right side flap, forming a seam running down the middle of

the steak. Repeat with the remaining steaks and fillings. The steaks should now be packages with the cheese, olives, tomato and basil wrapped up inside. Very gently give the joined edges of the steak a bit of a beating to help seal them together. Wrap the steaks, individually, in plastic wrap and put them in the fridge for an hour to help set the packages.

To make the caper sauce, put all the ingredients, except the olive oil, in a blender and pulse until you have a smooth liquid paste.

Heat a little olive oil in a frying pan over medium heat. Pour the sauce into the pan and cook, stirring, for about 5 minutes, then turn down the heat and simmer for about 20 minutes, stirring occasionally. Taste for seasoning and adjust as needed.

Put the flour on a plate and season with salt and pepper and any other spices you'd like to add. Dredge the pork packages one at a time in the seasoned flour, gently shaking off any excess, dip in the beaten egg to coat and then press in the breadcrumbs, turning to cover both sides completely.

Pour some olive oil into a frying pan, to about 1 cm (½ in) deep, then heat over medium–high heat until you can see it shimmering. Carefully add the pork parcels, seam side down first. Cook for a couple of minutes, then turn and cook for 2 minutes. Turn the heat down to medium and continue to fry and turn every couple of minutes, being careful not to burn. Cook until golden brown on both sides then remove and rest on paper towel to soak up any excess oil. Make sure that you cook the seam side well as it is two layers of the meat, one on top of the other, and you need to make sure the inside piece of meat is cooked through.

To serve, spoon some of the caper sauce onto each plate and place a pork sandwich on top, then spoon a little more sauce over. Serve with some roasted potatoes and steamed green beans or a salad.

Feeds 4

》》》》》》》》》》》》》》》》》》》》》》
TIP
Chilli powder, smoky paprika, ground sage and cumin are other spices that could be included.
》》》》》》》》》》》》》》》》》》》》》》

This is a rather rich pasta that is also glorious! Traditionally, it is made only with eggs, guanciale (cured and air-dried pig cheeks), cheese and black pepper. It is easier to use bacon as you can buy that anywhere, but I make it with pancetta because I love it and it is pretty easy to buy at your local gourmet deli. Better yet, buy a chilli pancetta if you want to add a bit of spice to this dish. To make this a more fulfilling meal I have added a couple of other ingredients. Broad beans when out of season can be bought frozen in supermarkets, which is great because you can just use what you need. When broad beans are in season, buy them fresh—for this recipe you will need around twenty whole pods to get the right amount of beans.

SPAGHETTI ALLA CARBONARA

1 packet fettuccine pasta
1 tablespoon butter
100 g (3½ oz) pancetta, cut into thin strips
1 small garlic clove, crushed
4 Swiss brown mushrooms, wiped clean and sliced
180 g (6¼ oz/1 cup) peeled fresh broad (fava) beans (or 750 g/1 lb 10 oz in the pod, or 350 g/12 oz frozen, then peel off the skin)

2 tablespoons flat-leaf (Italian) parsley, finely chopped, plus extra to serve (optional)
3 free-range eggs
70 g (2½ oz/⅔ cup) grated parmesan cheese plus extra to serve (optional)
freshly ground black pepper

Heat 2 litres (70 fl oz/8 cups) of water in a large saucepan with a generous pinch of salt over high heat. When it comes to the boil, add your pasta and cook, following the packet instructions until *al dente*.

While the water is coming to the boil put a frying pan over medium–high heat and melt the butter. Add the pancetta and fry for 5 minutes or until golden and slightly crispy. Add the garlic and cook for a couple of minutes, then add the mushrooms and broad beans and gently cook for another 5 or so minutes. Finally, add the parsley and mix through.

Beat the eggs together in a bowl. Mix in the cheese and a generous amount of pepper and then set aside.

When the pasta is cooked, turn off the heat and use tongs to transfer the pasta into the frying pan with the pancetta mix. Remove the pan from the heat, pour the egg and cheese mix over the top then mix together well. The heat from the pasta will cook the eggs so you want to move the mixture around to coat well and stop the eggs from scrambling. You should end up with a lovely rich pasta dish—if it is a little dry then add a teaspoon or two of the pasta water to loosen it up and give it a little more sauce.

Divide between four bowls and garnish with a little more parsley and a little more grated parmesan if you want.

Feeds 4

Nduja, pronounced 'en-doo-ya', is a spicy spreadable salami that hails from Calabria. It is a mixture of pork meat, roasted red peppers and spices that is then cured in a casing like salami, but remains soft like an uncooked sausage. Because it is cured you can eat it as is, either spreading it on grilled sourdough or in a roll with some provolone or over a pizza base. I absolutely love the flavour it adds to this pasta and I absolutely love to use the hot version as it really packs a kick! Additionally, I have read that nduja is considered an aphrodisiac ... so what are you waiting for ... get cooking!

NDUJA PORK PASTA

2 tablespoons olive oil

1 onion, diced

2 garlic cloves, finely chopped

120 g (4¼ oz) nduja paste (Calabrian spreadable salami paste—mild or hot)

500 g (1 lb 2 oz) minced (ground) pork

60 ml (2 fl oz/¼ cup) dry red wine

2 tins (400 g/14 oz each) chopped tomatoes

1 zucchini (courgette), diced

140 g (5 oz/1 cup) frozen peas

1 bunch basil

salt and freshly ground black pepper

500 g (1 lb 2 oz) penne rigate or rigatoni pasta*

100 g (3½ oz/1 cup) freshly grated parmesan cheese

Heat the olive oil in a large frying pan over medium–high heat. Add the onion and fry for a couple of minutes, then turn the heat down and cook for about 5 minutes until translucent. Add the garlic, stir through, and fry for another 5 minutes. Chop the nduja paste up and add to the pan, turn the heat back up to medium–high and stir well. Use the back of your wooden spoon to break down the paste (it is a firm sort of paste) and mix it through the onion mix. Add the pork mince and increase the heat to high. Again, using your wooden spoon, break the pork mince down so there are no big lumps of mince and mix to combine well with the paste. Cook for about 5 minutes, making sure the pork mince is browned. Add the red wine and mix through, then mix in the tomatoes. Bring the sauce to the boil then turn the heat down and simmer gently for 10 minutes. Next, add the zucchini, peas and about 15 torn basil leaves. Season, then let everything simmer gently for another 10–15 minutes, then it is ready to serve.

Meanwhile, cook the pasta in plenty of boiling water with a generous pinch of salt following the packet instructions, until *al dente*. Drain the pasta and then return to the pan. Put a ladleful of the sauce in with the pasta and mix through. Divide the pasta between each bowl, ladle over more nduja sauce, scatter over a tablespoon or two of the parmesan and serve.

Feeds 4–6

NOTE

This sauce is really quite big and robust, so I like to serve it with big pasta noodles. I buy Italian-made pasta that are like supersized rigatoni and are known as millerighe giganti pasta. You can buy these at specialist delis and there are various brands, but basically they are a tube of pasta about 3–4 cm (1½ in) long and about 1.5 cm (⅝ in) in diameter with long ridges or grooves in them which hold the sauce.

I was filming a cooking segment for my TV show at this beautiful winery in the King Valley in Victoria. Being at a winery, of course you cook with the wine, so I asked for a bottle for my slow-cooked goat and duly poured the whole lot into the pan. I did notice a slight look of shock and horror on the winemaker's face and later, while eating the goat I asked if he didn't like the way it was cooked. The winemaker said he loved the ragu, but he had never put that wine in a sauce before. I replied that it was a good wine to cook with, to which he said, 'It should be! We sell that for $100 a bottle!' I almost fell off my chair. They do say never cook with a wine you wouldn't drink, but I may have gone a little far with this one.

GOAT RAGU WITH RED WINE

1 shoulder baby goat, boned (to yield about 900 g/2 lb)
salt and freshly ground black pepper
plain (all-purpose) flour, for dusting
2 tablespoons olive oil
10 garlic cloves, peeled
8 French shallots (eschalots), peeled and the larger ones halved lengthways

3 tomatoes, roughly chopped
2 bay leaves
1 bottle dry red wine (I use sangiovese)
85 g (3 oz/½ cup) sultanas (golden raisins)
80 g (2¾ oz/½ cup) pine nuts, toasted
30 g (1 oz/½ cup) chopped flat-leaf (Italian) parsley

Preheat the oven to 160°C (315°F) (fan-forced 140°C/275°F).

Season the goat with some salt and pepper, then dust with the flour, patting the excess off.

Heat the olive oil in a flameproof casserole dish over high heat. Add the goat and brown on both sides. Add the garlic and French shallots and cook for a few minutes, then add the tomato, bay leaves, wine and 1 tablespoon of pepper. Give it all a mix, taste and season as necessary. Cut a sheet of baking paper to just fit inside the dish and place it over the goat. Cover tightly with a lid or foil and bake in the oven for 2½–3 hours or until the meat is falling apart and you can pick pieces off it with your fingers.

Remove the meat from the sauce and use two forks to shred the meat. Use the back of a spoon to squash the garlic cloves into the sauce and stir them through. You should have enough liquid for the sauce, but if you have too much then simmer the sauce to reduce it; if you don't have enough, then add a little water and simmer to incorporate it into the flavours. Put the meat back in the dish with the sultanas, pine nuts and parsley. Put the dish on the stovetop over gentle heat and bring to a simmer to heat the meat through.

You can serve this on pasta, rice or, even better, homemade gnocchi.

Feeds 6

I like to cook this dish at public cooking demos to teach people how easy it is to do a little bit of home smoking and show how delicious the result can be. Of course, I have to brine the fillet at home as the meat sits in the brine for several days. I also use this brine to smoke lamb rack and fish fillets—although for fish you only need to leave them in the brine for a couple of hours. The smoked eye fillet goes brilliantly with my lentil, parsley and tomato salad on page 100, you have been warned!

TEA-SMOKED BRINED EYE FILLET

200 g (7 oz) salt
200 g (7 oz) brown sugar
20 black peppercorns
3 bay leaves
3 pieces lemon rind, pith removed
660 ml (23 fl oz) dark ale or porter or stout

1 beef eye fillet (about 550–600 g/1 lb 4 oz–1 lb 5 oz)

Smoke Mix
40 g (1½ oz/½ cup) black tea leaves
100 g (3½ oz/½ cup lightly packed) brown sugar
110 g (3¾ oz/½ cup) medium-grain white rice

Put the salt, sugar, peppercorns, bay leaves and lemon rind in a large pot and pour over 1 litre (35 fl oz/4 cups) of boiling water. Stir and then add 2 litres (70 fl oz/8 cups) of cold water and the beer and stir again. Put the pot in the fridge to bring down the temperature. Once the brine is cold, place the eye fillet in—it should be completely covered by the brine—cover the pot with plastic wrap and place in the fridge for 2–3 days, turning the fillet each day.

Remove the fillet, pat dry with paper towel and then place on a wire rack sitting over a plate. Put the plate in the fridge uncovered for 1 day to dry out—this forms a pellicle (skin) which allows the smoke to stick to the meat.

To make the smoke mix, combine all the ingredients in a bowl well.

Line a wok with three layers of foil and pour in the smoke mix. Turn the heat to high and wait for the mix to begin to smoke, then put a wire rack in the wok and place the eye fillet on the rack. Cover tightly and once the smoke is really going turn the heat down a little to medium–high. Smoke the eye fillet until it reaches an internal temperature of 63–67°C (145–153°F). Depending on the thickness of the meat this may take anywhere from 25 to 35 minutes. In fact, try to buy one that has a uniform thickness from end to end, that way when you cook it you won't end up with a dry overcooked thin end and an underdone thick end.

Remove the fillet from the wok and leave to rest for 15–20 minutes—this will relax the meat and make it easier to slice—then slice the meat into 5 mm (¼ in) slices. You can either serve this on one large platter which looks great, or on individual plates—I like the large oval or long platter idea with lentil salad down the middle of the plate in a kind of long oblong shape. Either way, enjoy!

Serves 4–6

I have often seen people serve a side of pasta with a steak and never really understood it until I made this dish. I am not a fan of macaroni and cheese, something people often pair with a steak, but I guess if I was going to cook a macaroni and cheese this is how I would do it. That said, this is definitely not a mac and cheese, but rather a wonderful four-cheese pasta with a twist which you could cook and eat on its own, but it does go great with a beautifully cooked steak.

PASTA AI QUATTRO FORMAGGI & SCOTCH FILLET

1 beef scotch fillet (about 800 g–1 kg/1 lb 12 oz–
   2 lb 4 oz), tied to keep its round shape
salt and freshly ground black pepper
60 ml (2 fl oz/¼ cup) olive oil
60 ml (2 fl oz/¼ cup) brandy
2 tablespoon unsalted butter, plus extra if needed
1 brown onion, chopped
2 garlic cloves, chopped
90 g (3¼ oz/1 cup) chopped Swiss brown
   mushrooms
90 g (3¼ oz/1 cup) chopped button mushrooms

1 bunch enoki mushrooms, stems trimmed
30 g (1 oz/1⅓ cup) chopped flat-leaf (Italian) parsley
330 ml (11¼ fl oz/1⅓ cups) pouring cream
150 ml (5 fl oz) stout
500 g (1 lb 2 oz) penne pasta
70 g (2½ oz) cow's cheddar
70 g (2½ oz) goat's cheddar
70 g (2½ oz) blue cheese
70 g (2½ oz) triple cream brie cheese
pinch of white pepper

Preheat the oven to 200°C (400°F) (fan-forced 180°C/350°F).

Season the scotch fillet generously with salt and pepper. Heat 2 tablespoons of the olive oil in a frying pan over high heat and when smoking put the fillet in and brown well on all sides—this should take around 6–8 minutes. Once well caramelised, add the brandy and stand back—if the pan is hot enough the brandy will ignite. If you are cooking with gas you can tip the pan sideways so the brandy fumes can be ignited by the gas. The flames can go quite high, but don't worry they will not burn for long and it does look rather spectacular! Transfer the fillet to a roasting tin and cook for about 25 minutes. The internal temperature of the meat should be about 60–62°C (140–144°F) for a medium–rare result. Remove the meat from the oven and place on a plate, loosely cover with foil and rest in a warm spot for 10 or so minutes before carving into 5 mm (¼ in) slices.

While the meat is in the oven and using the same pan you browned the scotch fillet in, heat the remaining oil and butter over medium–high heat. When foaming, add the onion and cook down for several minutes, then add the garlic and cook for a further 3–5 minutes. Add all the mushrooms, mix well and cook for 10 minutes—if the pan becomes too dry, then add another tablespoon of butter. Add the parsley and stir through, then add the cream and the beer. Mix well and bring to the boil, then turn the heat down to medium and simmer for 8 minutes.

Fill a large saucepan with water, add a pinch of salt and bring to the boil. Add the penne pasta and cook following the packet instructions, until *al dente*.

Grate the firm cheeses and cut up the soft ones, then add to the simmering mushroom sauce mixture. Stir well to combine and continue to cook until the cheeses melt, then add the white pepper and stir. When the pasta is cooked strain and add to the sauce. Mix well to coat the pasta completely.

To serve, place the carved scotch fillet down one side of a large serving platter and then pile the pasta down the other side of the platter. Garnish with a little chopped parsley and serve in the middle of the table with a salad for everyone to help themselves.

Feeds 6

A WORD ON STEAK

When I told people I was writing this book many asked me to include some info on how to cook a good steak. Well, my view is if you really want to learn to cook a good steak all you have to do is cook some steaks and learn from your mistakes ... or should that be mis-steaks! I have three pieces of advice to help you along the way:

1. Start very hot then turn the heat down—either on the barbecue or in a chargrill pan. Season your steak with salt and black pepper, oil your pan or barbecue plate and when very hot place the steak on. Cook for about 2 minutes and then turn over and cook for another 2 minutes or so. Now turn the heat down from high to a medium–high and continue to cook until done to your desired level. See point 3 regarding turning your steak.

2. Use your fingers—by this I mean poke your steak as it cooks to feel how it is cooking and for when it is done to your desired level. A very very soft steak is most probably raw. A very soft steak that has been cooking for a couple of minutes on both sides will be rare. A steak that feels soft will be medium–rare. Soft with a bit of firmness will be medium and a steak that feels firmish will be medium to well, and a steak that feels quite firm will be well done! Remember, the steak will continue to cook after you take it off the heat so if you take it off when it is perfectly medium–rare, chances are it will be medium when you tuck into it. The trick is to take it off before it gets to your desired doneness and let it finish off the heat.

3. Turn your steak as many times as you want! Some chefs say you should only turn your steak once, others have said you should turn it every 20 seconds! I personally am a three to five times turner depending on the thickness of the steak—that is, I put the steak on the grill and turn it over three times then take it off just before it is cooked to my liking and let it finish on the plate; and if it is a really thick rib eye then I tend to turn it over five times. Just find out what works for you!

If you follow these three points you will learn to cook the perfect steak in no time. And lastly a word on resting ... again, like how many times you turn, it's a personal choice. As far as I'm concerned, the time it takes to put my steak on a plate along with some veggies or salad and carry said plate to table is a long enough rest for me!

How is this for sticking my neck out—if you follow this recipe you will get Really Crispy-Skinned Pork Belly! Pork skin can be a little temperamental at times and no matter what fool-proof method you follow it still won't do what it is supposed to do—turn in to magnificent crackle! Well this recipe works! You do need an oven that will get really hot so if you don't have one cook this at a neighbour's house, the only problem with that is you will have to share the crackle with them!!

REALLY CRISPY-SKINNED PORK BELLY

1 pork belly (about 1–1.5 kg/2 lb 4 oz–3 lb 5 oz)
2 tablespoons olive oil
2 teaspoons salt
2 teaspoons sichuan peppercorns, dry-roasted in a frying pan then crushed using a mortar and pestle
1 teaspoon celery salt

1 teaspoon fennel powder
1 teaspoon chilli powder
1 teaspoon garlic powder
1 teaspoon paprika
½ teaspoon freshly ground black pepper
1 teaspoon ground cumin
½ teaspoon salt

Preheat the oven to 250°C (500°F) (fan-forced 230°C/450°F).

Place the pork belly, skin side up, in a large roasting tin. Using a very sharp knife or a Stanley knife (box cutter), score the pork belly well unless your butcher has already done so. Pour 1 tablespoon of the olive oil over the skin and then rub the salt into the skin. Turn the belly over so the skin is facing down.

Combine the rest of the ingredients in a mixing bowl and then rub into the meat—do not rub it on the skin nor do you want oil on the meat. Make sure the meat is well coated with the spice rub. Use a paper towel to wipe any excess spice rub off the roasting tin and then place the pork into the hot oven.

Cook for 30 minutes then turn the heat down to 170°C (325°F) (fan-forced 150°C/300°F) and cook for another 1½ hours. Turn the pork belly over so the skin is up and turn the oven back up to 250°C (fan-forced 230°C) and cook for 10–20 minutes or until the skin is super crispy. Remove from the oven and place on a cutting board. Cut along the direction of the scored skin (top to bottom) in about 3 cm (1¼ in) strips, then cut these in half.

This is addictive and very tempting to just eat it on its own, however, it goes great with a rice salad (see page 97), warm potato salad (see page 102), 'slaw (see page 83) or soft salad (see page 96), and of course a cold beer!

Feeds 4 as a main or 8 as an entrée

This is a great little marinade for veal, and also for pork chops or medallions. If I am using pork I substitute the rosemary for fresh sage leaves and also add some roasted and crushed sichuan peppercorns to spice up the marinade.

BEER-MARINATED BARBECUED VEAL RIB-EYE

60 ml (2 fl oz/¼ cup) wheat beer
1 tablespoon sesame oil
juice of 1 lemon (about 2 tablespoons)
¼ red onion, finely diced
2 teaspoons chilli sauce
3 tablespoons chopped coriander (cilantro) leaves

1 tablespoon chopped rosemary
1 tablespoon chopped thyme
1 teaspoon dijon mustard
salt and freshly ground black pepper
4 veal rib-eye steaks on the bone

Mix all the ingredients together, except the steaks, in a baking dish large enough to hold the rib-eyes. Put the steaks in the marinade and make sure they are well coated. Cover the dish with plastic wrap and then leave to marinate for at least 2 hours or even overnight.

Preheat your barbecue grill to high. Wipe the grill with a little olive oil and then place the rib-eyes on the grill. Cook for about 5 minutes, then turn and cook for about 5 minutes more. Turn the heat down to medium, turn the steaks over and cook until you see blood 'sweating' from the upturned sides of the steaks. Turn the steaks over and cook until done to your liking. The timing of the cooking will depend on how large the rib-eyes are and how thick, so keep checking the doneness by how they feel to the touch—very soft to the touch is rare, soft with some spring back is medium–rare, soft with some firmness is medium and firm is well done.

Serve with my spring salad on page 225.

Feeds 4

Cooking chicken on the bone is the best way to go for flavour and tenderness, and cooking it on the barbecue is fantastic for that smoky charred flavour! I know some people don't like to eat the skin, but do the chicken a favour and cook it with the skin on as this will add flavour to the meat and protect it from drying out. And then if you don't want to eat the skin, give it to me!

BEER AND HERB-MARINATED CHICKEN

60 ml (2 fl oz/¼ cup) olive oil
60 ml (2 fl oz/¼ cup) lemon juice
125 ml (4 fl oz/½ cup) good quality craft beer
2 tablespoons soy sauce
2 garlic cloves, crushed
1 red chilli, chopped
2 spring onions (scallions), finely chopped

1 teaspoon Mexican chilli powder
¼ teaspoon sugar
15 g (½ oz/¼ cup) chopped basil
15 g (½ oz/½ cup) chopped flat-leaf (Italian) parsley
15 g (½ oz/¼ cup) chopped coriander (cilantro) leaves
freshly ground black pepper
1 free-range chicken (about 1.7 kg/3 lb 12 oz)

Combine all of the ingredients except the chicken in a mixing bowl, stir and then set aside while you prepare the chicken.

Cut down either side of the backbone of the chicken using kitchen scissors and remove—reserve for making chicken stock. Turn the chicken over so the breast is facing up and use the palms of your hands to press down firmly on the breastbone so it breaks and the chicken is splayed out flat. Use a sharp knife to cut the chicken in half, each with a leg and a breast. Score the flesh four or five times on each half—this allows the marinade to get into the meat. Put the chicken in a large non-metallic dish, breast side down, and spoon some of the marinade over, then turn the halves over and pour the rest of the marinade over the top of the chicken. Use your hands to rub the herbs over the chicken and into the cuts you made when you scored the chicken, then leave to marinate in the fridge for at least an hour, spooning the marinade over the chicken every 15 minutes or so.

Heat your barbecue grill for 15 minutes to medium–high with the lid on, then place the chicken halves on the grill skin side down, cover, and cook for 10 minutes. Turn the chicken over, cover and cook for another 10 minutes, spooning some marinade over the top. Turn over again (skin side down) spoon on some more marinade, turn the heat down to medium and cook for about 10–15 minutes, spooning some more marinade over after 10 minutes. Turn the chicken over again and cook for 15–20 minutes until the chicken is cooked through—if you have any marinade left tip it on.

Serve with warm potato salad (see page 102), rice salad (see page 97) or my soft salad (see page 96).

Feeds 4

Okay, it's not really a veal parma as a parma is generally considered to be crumbed and then shallow-fried with a tomato-based sauce and cheese chucked on the top. It's not really a saltimbocca alla romana either, as for that dish you normally roll the veal with sage and prosciutto inside and cook in white wine. Lastly, it is not veal scallopini as more often than not that is done with butter, white wine and mushrooms. So what is it? Well, delicious for one and, secondly, my homage to all three Italian dishes and a wonderful cut of meat.

VEAL PARMA

4 veal escalopes (about 120 g/4¼ oz each)
2 tablespoons olive oil
2 garlic cloves, finely chopped
4 anchovy fillets, chopped
1–2 red bird's red eye chillies, finely chopped
1 tablespoon baby capers
1 tablespoon plain (all-purpose) flour
1 tablespoon tomato paste (concentrated purée)
1 tin (400 g/14 oz) chopped tomatoes

60 ml (2 fl oz/¼ cup) red wine
3 tablespoons roughly chopped Spanish stuffed green olives
1 tablespoon chopped basil
½ teaspoon finely chopped sage
freshly ground black pepper
4 slices prosciutto
45 g (1½ oz) parmesan cheese

If the veal is a little thick you can put each piece between two pieces of plastic wrap and use a meat mallet or a rolling pin to gently beat it so that it stretches out to around 5 mm (¼ in) thick, then set aside.

Heat the olive oil in a frying pan over medium–high. Add the garlic, anchovy and chilli and stir through. When it starts to sizzle, turn the heat down to medium and add the capers, then cook, stirring for several minutes, so that the anchovy melts and all the flavours combine. Sprinkle some flour over the veal to very lightly coat both sides. Turn the heat back up to high and add the veal to the pan, pushing the capers, garlic and chilli to the side so the veal makes contact with the pan. Cook for a couple of minutes on one side and then turn and cook for a further 2–3 minutes on the other. Remove the veal from the pan and set aside on a plate. The veal should be not quite cooked when you take it out as it will be added to the sauce to finish off.

Add the tomato paste to the pan and stir through for a minute or so, then add the chopped tomatoes and stir through. Add the red wine, olives, basil and sage, then bring to a simmer. Taste for seasoning and add freshly ground black pepper—because of the capers, anchovies and olives I don't think you will need to add any salt. Simmer gently for 10–15 minutes to allow the flavours to combine, then add the veal back to the sauce to warm through.

Put a veal escalope on each plate, drape with a piece of prosciutto, spoon a generous amount of sauce over the top, then shave or grate some parmesan over it all and serve with some freshly made polenta and soft salad (page 96).

Feeds 4

Ah, the good old humble steak and kidney pie. Some people love to hate them and others love to eat them. This one has a little bit of a twist designed to soften the hearts of those who think they hate kidneys by adding some sweetness and spice, and a lovely maltiness from Belgian ale. Cut the kidneys into a small dice and you still get the lovely kidney flavour but it's balanced by all of the other ingredients. That's the point of cooking, really, combining flavours to make something more than the sum of its parts. This will become more than a steak and kidney pie, this will become your favourite pie!

STEAK AND KIDNEY PIE

80 ml (2½ fl oz/⅓ cup) olive oil, plus extra
   for greasing
1 red onion, sliced
3 garlic cloves, finely chopped
120 g (4¼ oz) chilli pancetta, cut into thin strips
1 tablespoon finely chopped rosemary
1 tablespoon finely chopped thyme
250 g (9 oz) lamb kidneys, fat removed, cut into
   small cubes
750 g (1 lb 10 oz) blade steak
75 g (2⅔ oz/½ cup) plain (all-purpose) flour
1 teaspoon salt
½ teaspoon freshly ground black pepper
1 teaspoon paprika

250 ml (9 fl oz/1 cup) beef stock
330 ml (11¼ fl oz/1⅓ cups) strong Belgian ale (such
   as Leffe Radieuse)
1 cinnamon stick
200 g (7 oz/1 cup) diced tomatoes
75 g (2⅔ oz/½ cup) sultanas (golden raisins)
200 g (7 oz/1 cup) cubed eggplant (aubergine)
90 g (3¼ oz/1 cup) chopped Swiss brown
   mushrooms
olive oil, for frying
1–2 sheets shortcrust pastry
1 sheet puff pastry
1 free-range egg, beaten

Preheat the oven to 180°C (350°F) (fan-forced 160°C/315°F).

Heat 1 tablespoon of the olive oil in a large flameproof casserole dish over medium–high. Add the onion and cook until translucent, and then add the garlic and pancetta and continue to cook for another 5 minutes or so before adding the chopped herbs and the kidneys. Cook for about 5 minutes, stirring to combine, then remove the dish from the heat, transfer the mixture into a bowl and set aside covered, to keep warm.

Meanwhile, cut the beef into roughly 2 cm (¾ in) cubes. Put the flour into a plastic bag and season with the salt, pepper and paprika. Add the beef and shake the bag to coat well. Put 1 tablespoon of oil into the empty casserole dish and brown the beef in batches, making sure to shake off the excess flour and adding more olive oil between each batch. Place the cooked meat in a bowl.

Deglaze the dish with half the beef stock, stirring vigorously and scraping the bottom of the pan to loosen all the flavour burnt on when browning the meat. Add 100 ml (3½ fl oz) of the beer and continue to stir and scrape to combine the liquid and the scrapings. Return the browned beef to the dish and stir to combine. Add the onion and kidney mixture, then add the remaining beef stock and about 150 ml (5 fl oz) of the beer and bring to the boil. Add the cinnamon stick, taste for seasoning and add salt and pepper as needed. Cut out a circle of baking paper so it fits snugly on top of the meat and seals the side of the dish, place on top then cover with a lid. Place the casserole dish in the oven and cook for 40 minutes. Remove from the oven, check the meat, add the tomato, sultanas, mushrooms and eggplant, give everything a good stir then put the baking paper and lid back on and cook for another 20–30 minutes or until the meat is tender and pulls apart easily. Do not overcook as this will dry the meat out. If you still have a lot of liquid in the pan, remove all the solids and increase the heat to reduce the sauce to your desired consistency—it should be unctuous and thick. Once reduced, put the solids back in, except the cinnamon stick. Remove from the heat and set aside to cool.

Increase the oven temperature to 200°C (400°F) (fan-forced 180°C/350°F).

Grease a 22 cm (8½ in) springform cake tin with a little olive oil. Roll the shortcrust pastry out between two sheets of baking paper large enough to cover the base and side of your tin. Line the tin with the pastry and trim any excess pastry. Cover with plastic wrap and chill for 20 minutes. Line the pastry shell with a piece of crumpled baking paper and pour in some baking beads or uncooked rice or beans and blind bake for 15 minutes, then remove the paper and beads and return to the oven for another 10–15 minutes or until lightly golden.

Increase the oven to 220°C (415°F) (fan-forced 200°C/400°F).

Fill your pie base with the cool meat mixture, then brush the sides of the baked shortcrust pastry so that the puff pastry lid will seal. Roll the puff pastry lid over the pie and press the sides down to seal. Trim off any excess pastry, brush the top with the beaten egg and then cut a cross in the top centre of your pie to allow the steam to escape. Cook for about 30 minutes, keeping an eye on the pie so that it doesn't burn. When the pastry is golden brown and crispy the pie is cooked.

Feeds 6–8

I love corned beef! I will often just cook one up and then keep it in the fridge and cut slices off it for sandwiches with lashings of hot mustard—really clears the sinuses! You can also fry some slices in a hot frying pan and then crack a couple of eggs in, and there's breakfast.

CORNED BEEF WITH MUSTARD SAUCE

1 piece of corned beef (about 1 kg/2 lb 4 oz)
6 cloves
1 large brown onion, peeled
1 large carrot, chopped into 4 pieces
15 black peppercorns
2 bay leaves
2 tablespoons malt vinegar
2 pieces lemon rind, pith removed
4 potatoes, peeled and cut into quarters
1 bunch baby carrots, cleaned
4 pieces Jap or butternut pumpkin (winter squash)

75 g (2⅔ oz/1 cup) thickly sliced red cabbage
75 g (2⅔ oz/1 cup) thickly sliced green cabbage

Mustard Sauce
1 tablespoon unsalted butter
1 tablespoon plain (all-purpose) flour
185 ml (6 fl oz/¾ cup) milk
185 ml (6 fl oz/¾ cup) corned beef cooking liquor
1 tablespoon dijon mustard
1 tablespoon wholegrain mustard
salt and freshly ground black pepper

Put the meat in a large saucepan and cover with cold water. Press the cloves into the onion and place in the water along with the carrot, peppercorns, bay leaves, vinegar and lemon rind. Bring to the boil, then turn down to a gentle simmer, skimming any scum off the surface every now and then. The meat should be cooked in 1¼ hours—if you have a meat thermometer the internal temperature should reach around 68–70°C (about 160°F). Remove from the pan and keep warm.

About 50 minutes into the cooking time take three ladlefuls of cooking liquor out of the pan and place in a separate saucepan. Put the potatoes, baby carrots and pumpkin in the pan, then top up with cold water to cover the veggies. Bring to the boil then reduce the heat and simmer until cooked. Drain and keep warm.

Meanwhile, make the mustard sauce. Place a small saucepan over medium–high heat, add the butter and when it begins to foam add the flour and whisk to combine. Continue to stir for a couple of minutes—but make sure not to colour or burn it. Gradually add the milk, stirring all the time, and then gradually add the corned beef cooking liquor and keep whisking—you may not need to add it all. Add both mustards and continue to stir. Taste and adjust the seasoning.

When you take the meat out of the cooking liquor put the cabbage into the pan and turn the heat up. Cook the cabbage for about 3–4 minutes.

To serve, slice the meat and dip it back into the hot cooking liquor to warm it. Serve individually, or place the meat and vegetables on a large serving platter in the middle of the table for people to help themselves.

Feeds 4–6

Pho soup is all the rage at the moment and for very good reason—it is absolutely delicious! There are two secrets to this Vietnamese soup: really good quality, fresh ingredients and a great stock. For an authentic pho soup you need to simmer beef bones over several days to get the complexity and depth of flavour. My version takes a few shortcuts but still tastes great.

EASY PHO SOUP

1 large piece ginger (about 6 cm/2½ in), unpeeled and halved lengthways
1 brown onion, unpeeled and halved
5 star anise
5 cloves
1 cinnamon stick
1 teaspoon fennel seeds
1 teaspoon coriander seeds
4 cardamom pods, cracked slightly
1 teaspoon black peppercorns
3 litres (105 fl oz/12 cups) beef stock
2 tablespoons fish sauce, plus extra to serve

2 tablespoons lime juice
1 tablespoon grated palm sugar (jaggery)
500 g (1 lb 2 oz) beef rump, sirloin or eye fillet
400 g (14 oz) vermicelli rice noodles
1 bunch baby bok choy (pak choy), trimmed
2 red bird's-eye chillies, thinly sliced
4 spring onions (scallions), sliced on the diagonal
handful of Vietnamese mint leaves, torn
handful of basil leaves, torn
handful of coriander (cilantro) leaves, torn
handful of bean sprouts
lime wedges, to serve

Preheat your grill (broiler) to high. Place the ginger and onion, skin side up on a baking tray and grill for about 10 minutes, turning every couple of minutes and allow the onion and ginger to char. Remove from under the heat and set aside.

Put the dried spices in a frying pan and dry-fry, stirring constantly, until fragrant and smoking slightly then remove from the heat.

Put the stock into a large stockpot, add the dry-fried spices and the onion. Put the pot over high heat and bring to the boil, then reduce the heat, cover and simmer gently for 1 hour.

Pour the stock into a colander placed over a large bowl and then discard the solids—you should have about 2.5 litres (87 fl oz/10 cups) of stock. Top up with boiling water if necessary. Return the stock to the pot and return to the heat. Add the fish sauce, lime juice and palm sugar and simmer for another 30 minutes.

Meanwhile, put the beef in the freezer and partially freeze, then remove and slice very, very thinly until you have about 450 g (1 lb) or so of thinly sliced meat. Make sure to use the leftover steak for something else.

Bring 1.5 litres (52 fl oz/6 cups) of water to the boil in a saucepan, then drop the rice noodles in and stir. Turn the flame off and leave the noodles to cook.

Bring the soup to the boil, add the bok choy and cook for 2–3 minutes. Divide the noodles between serving bowls, add the meat and bok choy, ladle in some soup and garnish with chilli and spring onions. Serve with the herbs, bean sprouts, fish sauce and lime wedges on the side, and more chilli and spring onions if you like.

Feeds 4–6

I really like to make my own curry pastes as I enjoy the process and it means I know what is in them in terms of salts, sugars and no preservatives, and they tastes better than anything you buy in a jar because they are utterly and completely fresh! That said, when I came to editing this recipe I looked at it and went 'Struth. Nineteen ingredients!' That is a lot I know, but I would urge you to have a go—it's not hard or complicated, you just need to commit to the process and have fun.

OVEN-ROASTED TANDOORI LAMB LEG

2 tablespoons coriander seeds
1 tablespoon cardamom seeds
1½ teaspoons ground cumin
1½ teaspoons chilli powder
1½ teaspoons ground turmeric
1 teaspoon garam masala
1 teaspoon black mustard seeds
½ teaspoon salt
½ teaspoon freshly ground black pepper
¼ teaspoon sugar

4 garlic cloves, roughly chopped
2 cm (¾ in) piece ginger, roughly chopped
3 coriander (cilantro) roots, scraped and chopped
1 brown onion, roughly diced
1 long green chilli, chopped
juice of ½ lemon (about 1 tablespoon)
3 tablespoons chopped coriander (cilantro) leaves
4 tablespoons Greek-style yoghurt
1 lamb leg (about 1.5 kg/3 lb 5 oz)

Dry-fry the coriander seeds and cardamom seeds in a clean dry frying pan over high heat until fragrant and smoking, then using a mortar and pestle grind into a powder. Tip the rest of the dry ingredients into the mortar and grind to combine well. Pour the dry mix into a bowl and set aside.

Put the garlic and ginger into the mortar and break down using the pestle, then grind in the coriander roots. Add the onion and bash together for several minutes. Add half the dry mix and continue to grind away. Add the chopped chilli and continue to work away. Next, add the lemon juice and the rest of the dry mix and grind into a rough paste, then mix through the coriander and yoghurt.

Place the lamb on a cutting board and make four or five cuts about 2 cm (¾ in) deep along the leg on the diagonal, then make four or five cuts on the other diagonal to form squares. Turn the leg over and repeat the cuts on the other side. Put the lamb leg in a baking dish and smother all over with the tandoori paste, rubbing it into the cuts. Cover with plastic wrap and marinate in the fridge for several hours, however, you need to bring it to room temperature before cooking.

Preheat the oven to 170°C (325°F) (fan-forced 150°C/300°F).

Cover the lamb with foil and put the baking dish in the oven and cook for 1½ hours. Remove the foil, turn the heat up to 200°C (400°F) (fan-forced 180°C/350°F) and cook for a further 30 minutes or until well coloured.

Serve with steamed rice or whatever you fancy.

Feeds 6–8

I first made this stew when I was filming my TV show in Kenya. Of course, being in a different country meant there were different customs and ingredients. The gentleman I was cooking with who was the head chef at the lodge we were staying at gave me some chillies to use in the stew which I assumed would be the same as the ones I use in Australia—they were not, they were quite a bit hotter and let's just say there was much sweating going on around the table at tasting time!

RICH SPICED LAMB STEW

80 ml (2½ fl oz/⅓ cup) olive oil
1 large red onion, sliced
4 garlic cloves, roughly chopped
1 tablespoon ground cumin
1 tablespoon sweet paprika
1 tablespoon chilli powder
600 g (1 lb 5 oz) deboned lamb leg, cut into roughly
   2 cm (¾ in) cubes
250 ml (9 fl oz/1 cup) Belgian double ale
1 red bird's-eye chilli, sliced (or to taste; I use up to
   4 chillies to make this really quite hot!)

45 g (1⅔ oz/¼ cup) sultanas (golden raisins)
6 semi-dried dates (such as medjool)
1 cinnamon stick
15 g (½ oz/¼ cup) chopped coriander (cilantro)
7 g (¼ oz/¼ cup) chopped flat-leaf (Italian) parsley
3 roma (plum) tomatoes, cut into 6 wedges each
45 g (1⅔ oz/1 cup) sliced kale
salt and freshly ground black pepper

Heat the olive oil in a large deep-sided frying pan or flameproof casserole dish that has a lid over medium–high heat, then add the onion and garlic, and fry, stirring often, for 8–10 minutes. Add the cumin, paprika and chilli powder, stirring to combine, and continue to fry for a couple of minutes. Increase the heat to high, add the lamb and stir well to coat with the spice mix, then brown for about 10 minutes. Stir in the beer and 150 ml (5½ fl oz) of water, then stir in the sliced chillies, sultanas, dates and cinnamon. Season, then add the fresh herbs. Turn down to a simmer, cover with the lid and cook for about 1½ hours or until the meat is quite tender. Check the meat after an hour or so.

   Add the tomato wedges and kale to the stew, stirring to combine, and simmer for a further 10 minutes. You may need to add a little extra water as the stew can become a little dry. It is meant to be a thick-dry style stew though, not a wet stew with lots of liquid.

   Serve on mashed potato or with boiled potatoes on the side or some couscous.

Feeds 4

WARNING: This recipe will challenge you, but it will also delight! Yes it is complicated; yes you will have to work hard to track down the correct chillies and yes you will have to work even harder to cook the dish. Will it be worth it? YES! Should you give it a go? ABSOLUTELY! Mole poblano is a traditional Mexican sauce created by a nun a couple of hundred years ago, or so the story goes. Mole is pronounced 'mol-ay'. There are several different styles of mole and they range in difficulty from sort of simple, using fifteen different ingredients, to very complex using twenty-five ingredients or more. Mole poblano is characteristically dark red or brown, rich, smoky, aromatic, slightly hot and thick. It was traditionally served with boiled turkey but nowadays you can serve it with whatever cut of meat you wish. You can buy the dried chillies at specialist stores, really good delis, farmers' markets or online.

TURKEY COOKED IN MOLE POBLANO

1 brown onion, unpeeled
2 garlic cloves, unpeeled
3 chipotle chillies (dried jalapeños, smoky–hot)
3 ancho chillies (earthy, mild)
3 mulato chillies (dark, sweet, mild)
2 mirasol chillies (hot)
40 g (1½ oz/¼ cup) blanched almonds
2 tablespoons sesame seeds
2 corn tortillas
1 tin (400 g/14 oz) chopped tomatoes
¼ teaspoon freshly ground black pepper
1 teaspoon ground coriander

¼ teaspoon ground cloves
½ teaspoon ground cinnamon
1 banana
250 ml (9 fl oz/1 cup) vegetable stock
60 ml (2 fl oz/¼ cup) olive oil
1 kg (2 lb 4 oz) turkey thighs, skin removed, cut into large chunks
50 g (1¾ oz) dark chocolate (85% cocoa)
salt and freshly ground black pepper
1 lime
4 tablespoons chopped coriander (cilantro) leaves

Preheat the grill (broiler) to high.

Cut the onion in half, leaving the skin on, and place it skin side up on a baking tray. Put the garlic cloves next to the onion and then grill until the onion skin is blackened and the garlic is soft. Remove from under the grill, peel and set aside.

Preheat the oven to 170°C (325°F) (fan-forced 150°C/300°F).

Cut the stems off the chillies, then cut down one side to open them up. Remove the seeds, then tear the chilli halves into smaller pieces. Put the chilli skins in a non-stick frying pan over medium–high heat and using another heavy-based pan or egg slide press the skins down until toasted on one side. Turn them over and

when they begin to smoke slightly remove and place in a bowl. Cover the chillies with boiling water and place a plate on top to keep the chilli pieces submerged. Soak for at least 30 minutes.

To the same frying pan in which you toasted the chillies, add the blanched almonds and toast until they get some colour, then remove and set aside in a bowl. Put the sesame seeds in the pan and toast until brown, then put in the bowl with the almonds. Again, using the same pan, toast the tortillas, one at a time, until slightly coloured then remove and tear into pieces.

Put the almonds and sesame seeds in a food processor and blend until crushed, then add the onion and garlic and blend until smooth. Add the tomatoes, tortilla, spices, banana and stock, and blend until well combined, scraping down the sides. Pour the mixture into a bowl.

Add the soaked chillies to a blender along with about 125 ml (4 fl oz/½ cup) of the soaking liquid and blend until smooth. You will need to scrape down the side of the blender as you do this and you may need to add a little more soaking liquid so that you end up with a thick soupy texture. Add the tomato and spice mix and blend to combine well.

Heat half the olive oil in a large flameproof casserole dish over high heat. Add the turkey and brown well, seasoning with salt and black pepper. You will need to do this in two batches, adding the remaining oil for the second batch. Once brown add the mole sauce and stir well. Bring the sauce to the boil then add the chocolate and stir through so that it melts and combines evenly. Put a lid on the dish and put in the oven for about 1½ hours or until the meat is very tender.

When the meat is cooked squeeze the lime over and sprinkle with coriander, stir through the sauce and then serve.

Serve over rice garnished with some extra coriander and sesame seeds and some steamed zucchini (cougette) or beans.

Feeds 6

If you are like me and love the Tex-Mex set of flavours then this dish will become one of your staple cooks. It really is a simple dish to make—yes it takes a little bit of knife work but after you have done it once, you will be an expert the next time. It also has that wow factor as a dish as it is not often you come across it anywhere. You can also up the wow factor by using blue corn chips or a mix of blue and normal to get a speckled effect going on in the crumbs.

STUFFED CHICKEN MEXICAN STYLE WITH SALSA

500 g (1 lb 2 oz/2¼ cups) cream cheese

115 g (4 oz/½ cup) chopped pickled jalapeño chillies, reserve some pickling juice

4 large free-range skinless chicken breasts

2 packets gluten-free organic corn chips

75 g (2⅔ oz /½ cup) plain (all-purpose) flour

1 tablespoon paprika

1 tablespoon Mexican chilli powder

salt and freshly ground black pepper

2 free-range eggs, beaten

olive oil, for shallow-frying

Salsa

3 large tomatoes, peeled, seeded and diced

1 large red onion, finely diced

1 avocado, diced

1 long red chilli, finely diced

1 garlic clove, finely chopped

1 tablespoon chopped coriander (cilantro) leaves

juice of ½ lime (about 2 teaspoons)

salt

2 tablespoons olive oil

To make the salsa, mix the tomato, onion, avocado, chilli, garlic and coriander together in a bowl. Season with the lime juice and salt, then drizzle in the olive oil. Mix again and taste to check you are happy with the seasoning. Set aside.

Preheat the oven to 220°C (415°F) (fan-forced 200°C/400°F).

Heat the cream cheese in the microwave for about 10 seconds or so to soften it then put in a glass bowl. Mix through the chopped jalapeños and about 2 tablespoons of the pickling liquid to help soften the cheese. Once everything is combined have a taste to check the heat. If you want it hotter then add some more chopped jalapeños.

Carefully make a hole down the centre of the chicken breasts with a sharp knife, starting at the thick end of the breast and working towards the tail or thin end. Be very careful not to pierce the outside of the breast or take the hole all the way through—we are making a pocket lengthways through the breast to fill it with the cheese mixture.

Fill a piping (icing) bag with the cheese mixture and gently pipe it into the chicken pocket. As you fill the pocket, massage the cheese mixture so that it fills the hole, being careful not to split the chicken breast by forcing too much in. Make sure you fill the pocket so that it feels firm. Repeat with the other three breasts.

Put the corn chips in a food processor and blitz into fine crumbs then tip onto a plate. Season the flour with the paprika, chilli powder, salt and pepper, then dredge the stuffed chicken breasts in the flour shaking off any excess. Dip the breasts in the beaten egg making sure they are completely coated and then roll them in the corn chip crumbs, pressing down gently to coat well.

Pour some olive oil into a frying pan, about 1 cm (½ in) deep, then heat over medium–high heat until you can see it shimmering. Carefully add the chicken breasts and shallow-fry until they are golden brown on both sides. Remove from the frying pan, place on a baking tray and then put them in the oven for about 7 minutes. Remove the chicken from the oven and rest for a couple of minutes.

Serve the chicken on a plate with a generous serve of the salsa, some guacamole (page 65) and a side of fries.

Feeds 4

It's a strange thing to go out to a paddock and pick the goat you are going to eat—we don't mind catching a fish or picking a crab from the tank, but a baby goat? Well, luckily you only need to go down to your local farmers' market and buy a shoulder of goat off your specialist butcher, then go home and treat it with the respect it deserves. You could use lamb if you wanted instead of goat.

ITALIAN WHITE GOAT STEW

120 ml (4 fl oz) olive oil
1 brown onion, halved and sliced
1 red capsicum (pepper), cut into 1 cm (½ in) strips
4 garlic cloves, roughly chopped
100 g (3½ oz) pancetta, cut into thin strips
2 rosemary sprigs
75 g (2⅔ oz/½ cup) plain (all-purpose) flour
½ teaspoon salt
½ teaspoon freshly ground black pepper
1 teaspoon ground cumin
750 g (1 lb 10 oz) deboned goat leg, cut into chunks

125 ml (4 fl oz/½ cup) dry white wine
125 ml (4 fl oz/½ cup) chicken stock
3 tomatoes, roughly chopped
250 g (9 oz) teardrop or grape tomatoes
1 tin (400g/14 oz) chickpeas, drained and rinsed
180 g (6¼ oz/1 cup) kalamata olives
salt and freshly ground black pepper
1 small eggplant (aubergine), cut into 8 wedges
2 large zucchini (courgettes), each cut into
     quarters lengthways
2 tablespoons chopped flat-leaf (Italian) parsley

Preheat the oven to 180°C (350°F) (fan-forced 160°C/315°F).

Heat 2 tablespoons of the olive oil in a large flameproof casserole dish over high heat. Add the onion, capsicum, garlic, pancetta and rosemary and cook, stirring, for several minutes, then reduce the heat to medium and cook for a further 5 or so minutes. Remove this mixture from the dish and set aside.

Combine the flour, salt, pepper and cumin in a plastic bag and mix well, then add the goat and shake the bag to evenly coat. In the same dish as you fried the onion heat another 2 tablespoons of oil, then add the floured goat meat, shaking off the excess flour before you add the meat to the oil. You may need to brown the meat in batches and then return to the dish. When all the meat is browned, deglaze the pan with the white wine. Add the stock and return the onion mixture to the dish, stir, then mix through the chopped tomato and bring to a simmer. Cover the stew with baking paper, cover the dish with foil and then put the lid on. Cook in the oven for 1¼ hours.

Add the teardrop tomatoes, chickpeas and olives, stir, then taste for seasoning and add salt and black pepper as needed. Cook for a further 10 minutes or so.

Meanwhile, preheat the grill (broiler) or barbecue to medium–high.

Put the eggplant and zucchini wedges in a bowl and dress with the remaining oil, and season with a pinch of salt. Grill for about 10 minutes, turning often until charred and cooked. To serve, place two wedges of eggplant and two of zucchini on each plate, and garnish with a little chopped parsley. Serve with a bowl of polenta or potato mash.

Feeds 4

I had never made this dish in my life when I turned up to a very highly decorated and prestigious 'chef of the year' Sydney restaurant. We were shooting a cooking segment for my TV show and I had just happened to visit a sake brewery in outer western Sydney and a quail farm, so of course I thought 'quail and sake, why not!' Once I walked into the restaurant and realised what a big deal it was to be cooking there with the head chef I started to freak out and my producer made several comments regarding my sanity. The other chefs prepping for dinner were quite curious about what I was cooking and I reckon were taking bets on whether it was going to fail. I am proud (and relieved) to say it turned out to be delicious, so give it a go!

SAKE-GRILLED QUAIL WITH PEACH SALSA AND MISO EGGPLANT

4 boned jumbo quail (about 140 g/5 oz each)

Quail Marinade
125 ml (4 fl oz/½ cup) sake
125 ml (4 fl oz/½ cup) mirin
125 ml (4 fl oz/½ cup) soy sauce
125 ml (4 fl oz/½ cup) orange juice
2 teaspoons chopped pickled ginger
1 tablespoon caster (superfine) sugar
1 tablespoon finely chopped coriander (cilantro) leaves
½ teaspoon sesame oil

Peach Salsa
400 g (14 oz/2 cups) diced firm peach flesh
¾ red onion finely diced
2½ tablespoons finely chopped coriander (cilantro) leaves
2½ tablespoons sake
¾ teaspoon grated palm sugar
¾ red bird's-eye chilli, finely chopped
juice of 1 small lime (about 1 tablespoon)

White Miso Eggplant and Zucchini
2 small eggplants (aubergines), each cut into 6 wedges lengthways
3 large zucchini (courgettes), each cut into 4 wedges lengthways
peanut oil
60 ml (2 fl oz/¼ cup), plus 1 tablespoon extra, white miso paste
80 ml (2½ fl oz/⅓ cup) sake
80 ml (2½ fl oz/⅓ cup) mirin
1⅓ teaspoons caster (superfine) sugar
sesame seeds, to garnish

Most people think of cooking meat as generally using four main options—beef, lamb, chicken and pork—but there is so much more out there …

Mix the quail marinade ingredients together in a bowl, making sure the sugar is well dissolved, then pour over the quail and massage into the birds for a few minutes. Leave for 1–2 hours before cooking.

To make the peach salsa, combine the peach, onion and coriander in a bowl. In a separate bowl, combine the sake, palm sugar, chilli and lime juice and mix, making sure the sugar is completely dissolved in the dressing. Add the dressing to the bowl with the peach and mix well. Set aside.

Preheat your barbecue grill to medium–high.

Put the marinated quail on the grill and cook for a few minutes on either side— turning so they don't burn. When the quail are nicely coloured either put them in a hot oven for 5 minutes to finish cooking or turn the barbecue down and continue to cook over the grill until done.

Meanwhile, to make the white miso eggplant and zucchini, brush the wedges with a little peanut oil and then put them on the barbecue grill and cook until soft and coloured, turning every 4 minutes or so. You may need to brush the eggplant with some more oil after you turn it. Mix the miso paste, sake, mirin and sugar together in a bowl. When the eggplant and zucchini are almost finished cooking, brush them generously with the miso glaze. The eggplant and zucchini should be evenly coloured and quite soft when cooked through. When finished cooking, remove to a clean plate, brush with any remaining glaze and sprinkle with the sesame seeds.

To serve, place three pieces of eggplant and three pieces of zucchini on each plate, crossing them over to create some height, then lay a quail partially over the top. Serve the peach salsa to the side and spoon any pan juices from the quail over the top of the quail and around the plate.

Feeds 4

NOTE

You can get jumbo quail from specialist poultry stores often at major markets. They will debone them for you as well for a couple of extra dollars.

Most people use milk as an addition in their cooking, whether it be added to your mashed potatoes, your chowder, your ice cream or your mornay sauce. I had never really considered it as a main ingredient in the cooking of a dish. I first used it to make a milk-braised pork dish inspired by the classic Italian dish 'arrosto di maiale al latte' which was really delicious so I thought I would have a go at braising lamb in a similar way. It turned out the lady I cooked it for had been a vegetarian for four years and this was the first meat she had eaten in that time—and, yes, she said she liked it!

MILK-BRAISED LAMB WITH FENNEL

3 teaspoons fennel seeds
80 ml (2½ fl oz/⅓ cup) olive oil
1 kg (2 lb 4 oz) lamb leg or shoulder meat, cut into large chunks, trimmed of fat
salt and freshly ground black pepper
1 leek, white part only, sliced
2 small fennel bulbs, sliced
3 rosemary sprigs
2 dried bay leaves
1 garlic bulb, halved crossways
1 litre (35 fl oz/4 cups) milk
½ teaspoon ground nutmeg

Preheat the oven to 180°C (350°F) (fan-forced 160°C/315°F).

Place a small frying pan over high heat and add the fennel seeds. Dry-fry them, shaking the pan often, until they begin to smoke. Remove from the heat and grind them into a powder using a mortar and pestle.

Heat 1½ tablespoons of the olive oil in a flameproof casserole dish over high heat. Season the lamb with salt and pepper and when the oil is hot, brown the meat—you may need to do this in two batches, adding the same amount of olive oil for the second batch. While the meat is browning, season the meat with half the freshly ground fennel powder, do the same with the second batch. When the meat is browned remove it from the dish and set aside.

Heat the remaining olive oil in the dish, then add the leek and cook gently until fragrant and caramelised. Add the sliced fennel and cook for several minutes until wilted and fragrant.

Return the meat to the casserole dish along with any collected juices, add the rosemary, bay leaves and garlic and fry for a couple of minutes, stirring all the time. Add the milk and nutmeg, season with salt and pepper then bring just to the boil. Remove from the heat, cover with baking paper, put the lid on and transfer to the oven. Cook for about 1½ hours or until the meat is very tender. Once tender remove the lid and baking paper, turn the oven to high and cook until the top is golden and caramelised.

Serve on couscous with some steamed vegetables or my couscous and roast veggie salad on page 22 (although as that is written for a night in alone you will need to multiply the recipe by around 4).

Feeds 4–6

I am partial to the combination of smoky paprika, chillies, red kidney beans and tender meat—they work so well together and I reckon I could eat it all day. Even though the list of ingredients looks a little long, this stew is pretty straightforward to make. It is a great winter dish because of its heartiness and chilli bite, but then it is pretty good in autumn and spring as well!

TEX-MEX BEEF STEW

35 g (1¼ oz/¼ cup) plain (all-purpose) flour

6 tablespoons smoky paprika

½ teaspoon salt, plus extra to season

½ teaspoon freshly ground black pepper

1 beef scotch fillet (about 750 g/1 lb 10 oz), cut into 4 cm (1½ in) chunks

80 ml (2½ fl oz/⅓ cup) olive oil

1 red onion, halved lengthways, cut into 4 wedges

120 g (4¼ oz) chorizo, diced

2 celery stalks, chopped to yield about 50 g (1¾ oz)

3 garlic cloves, finely chopped

2 red bird's-eye chillies, sliced

1 red capsicum (pepper), sliced

1 tin (400 g/14 oz) chopped tomatoes

125 ml (4 fl oz/½ cup) dry red wine

375 ml (13 fl oz/1½ cups) beef stock

2 carrots, cut into 6 pieces each

360 g (12¾ oz) pumpkin (winter squash), cut into 12 pieces

2 zucchini (courgettes), halved lengthways and then cut into 1 cm (½ in) half-moon shapes

1 tin (400 g/14 oz) red kidney beans, drained, rinsed

1 teaspoon lemon thyme (or normal thyme)

2 tablespoons chopped flat-leaf (Italian) parsley

Preheat the oven to 170°C (325°F) (fan-forced 150°C/300°F).

Mix the flour, paprika, salt and pepper together in a plastic bag, add the beef and give it a good shake to coat. Remove the excess flour and set aside.

Heat 1 tablespoon of the olive oil in a flameproof casserole dish over high heat. Ad half the beef and brown on all sides then remove the meat to a bowl. Add another tablespoon of oil to the dish and brown the remaining meat, then transfer to the bowl and set aside.

Add the remaining olive oil to the dish, reduce the heat to medium–high and when hot add the onion and fry for a couple of minutes. Add the chorizo and fry, stirring for a couple of minutes. Add the garlic, red chilli, celery and capsicum and fry for a few more minutes before adding the tomatoes, wine and stock. Give everything a good mix and allow the liquid to come to the boil. Add the carrot, pumpkin, zucchini, kidney beans, browned beef and thyme, give everything a big stir to combine and bring the liquid up to a firm simmer. Season with salt and pepper and give it one final stir.

Put a lid on the dish, put the casserole in the oven and cook for about 1½ hours. If you decided to use a cheaper cut of meat such as shin or oyster blade then you may need to cook the meat for a couple of hours until it gets very tender. Check the meat after 1¼ hours and if the meat and vegetables are tender, serve in a bowl over rice or with some mashed potato. Garnish the stew with some freshly chopped parsley.

Feeds 4–6

You may have noticed that this is the biggest recipe I have written in this book and you may be thinking that it looks a little on the hard side to make. Well, let me just say that yes it is the biggest recipe I've written in this book, but it is not as hard as it looks. If you get your specialist poultry person to debone the duck for you the rest is pretty easy, and if I may say so, the results are well worth the effort. Of course, if you are looking to impress somebody then this is the dish that will do it.

DUCK BALLOTINE ON CELERIAC MASH WITH ORANGE SAUCE

500 g (1 lb 2 oz) minced (ground) pork
3 tablespoons chopped coriander (cilantro) leaves
2 tablespoons chopped sage
2 tablespoons chopped chervil
3 tablespoons chopped pimientos de padron
    (Spanish peppers or banana peppers from a jar)
rind of two oranges, pith removed, finely chopped
    (to yield about 1 tablespoon of zest)
60 g (2¼ oz) macadamia nuts, finely chopped
1 free-range egg
1 tablespoon Madeira
sea salt and freshly ground black pepper
olive oil, for frying
1 duck (about 2 kg/4 lb 8 oz)

Celeriac Mash
1 celeriac, peeled and cubed
pinch of salt
60 ml (2 fl oz/¼ cup) milk
2 tablespoons butter

Orange Sauce
55 g (2 oz/¼ cup) raw sugar
60 ml (2 fl oz/¼ cup) sherry vinegar
60 ml (2 fl oz/¼ cup) chicken stock
juice of 1 orange (about 2 tablespoons)
1 tablespoon Madeira
1 bay leaf
1 tablespoon butter

Place the pork mince, coriander, sage, chervil, peppers, orange zest, macadamia nuts, egg and Madeira in a large mixing bowl and give it all a good mix with your hands, making sure all of the ingredients are well combined. Season with salt and black pepper and mix again. Take about 2 teaspoons worth of the mixture, form it into a patty and cook it in a little olive oil in a frying pan. Taste the cooked patty for seasoning and adjust the raw mixture as necessary, then set aside the remaining raw mince mixture.

To prepare the duck you can do this the easy way or the hard way. The easy way is to go to a specialist poultry seller, buy a duck and ask them to debone it for you. Ask them to take the wing and leg bones out and keep the duck neck skin whole, or otherwise buy a duck neck skin as well. The hard way is, of course, buying a duck and deboning it yourself. It is not that hard, however, it does require patience and a very sharp knife, and unfortunately if you put a hole in the skin you will have to start again by buying another duck! ➜➜

◄━◄◄

Let's assume you went the smart route and got your duck deboned. Lay the duck carcass, skin side down, on a clean work surface. You should have a kind of square shape of skin with the breast and leg meat still attached, but no bones present. You need to gently peel the meat away from the skin using your hands, fingers and also a very sharp knife. Be careful to keep the breast meat whole. You can work your fingers between the meat and the skin and then get your knife in there and carefully cut just between the meat and the skin to free the meat. If there are any big fatty deposits, carefully cut them off also, but be very careful not to pierce the skin. If successful you should have a square of duck skin without any holes in it except for where the wing and thighbone came out—just use that flap of skin to fold over the hole. If you still have the duck neck skin attached you can cut that off to square up the skin.

Depending on how you removed the duck breast you will have two breasts still joined together or two separate breasts. Clean the breast meat up by separating the breasts and cutting away any excess fat or tendon, then cut each duck breast lengthways into three long pieces, trying to keep the pieces about equal size.

Lay the skin out flat on a large piece of plastic wrap with the outer skin side down. Spread the pork mixture on top of the skin about 1 cm (½ in) thick, making sure it is evenly spread all over the skin and also leaving about 1 cm (½ in) gap of skin not covered at the bottom edge (closest to you). Next, place the pieces of duck breast in the middle of the skin—lay three pieces down, then put two pieces on top of them and then lay the last piece of duck breast on the top. Using the plastic wrap, take the top edge and lift it up and over rolling the duck skin up like a sausage. The mince should roll over the duck breast forming a sausage casing around them—do not tuck the duck skin into the mince mix—the top edge of the skin should roll over and join the bottom edge of the skin which you can then fold over the top, closing the gap to form a sausage. Make sure you fold over the side ends so that they are closed. Roll up in plastic wrap and twist the ends tightly to form a good tight casing around the duck sausage. You can do this by rolling the duck on your work surface, holding either end of the plastic wrap so that it tightens into a cylinder, then put rubber bands over the twisted ends so they do not unravel. Wrap three or four times in extra pieces of plastic wrap so it is watertight and, if you want, you can tie the ends with string so they will not come undone when you poach it. Put the duck ballotine in the fridge for a couple of hours to allow the meat to set.

You may have some mince left over depending on the size of the duck, so take your whole duck neck that you bought and tie the skinny end shut using some kitchen string. Then stuff the pork mince mixture down into the duck neck and push down firmly so it is tight. Using kitchen string tie the top of the neck shut as close to the meat as you can and you will now have one duck sausage to cook later!

Place the ballotine into a large saucepan filled with boiling water, bring the water back to a simmer then cover the pan with the lid. Simmer for about 30–40 minutes or until the internal temperature of the ballotine reaches 62–65°C (144–149°F). Remove the cooked ballotine from the water, take out of the plastic wrap and pat dry with paper towel. Put a tea towel (dish towel) on a plate and then place the ballotine on top, then transfer to the fridge, keeping the ballotine uncovered for a couple of hours to dry out the skin—this helps the skin to crisp when you fry it.

Place a frying pan over high heat, add a little oil and when the oil starts to smoke add the ballotine to the pan. Keep an eye on the temperature of the pan as you don't want it too hot so as to burn the duck skin. Turn the duck to evenly colour, and cook until the skin is well coloured and crispy. Remove from the pan and rest, covered, on a plate.

Meanwhile, to make the celeriac mash, put the cubes of celeriac into a saucepan, cover with cold water, add a pinch of salt, then place over high heat and bring to the boil. Reduce the heat to medium so that the water is firmly simmering and cook until the celeriac is tender. Tip the celeriac and water into a colander to drain, then return the celeriac to the same pan and place over very low heat. Use a fork or a potato masher to mash the celeriac then add some milk and the butter—you may not need all the milk so add a little at a time. Continue to mash until the celeriac is smooth and the consistency is nice and fluffy. Season with salt and freshly ground black pepper.

To make the orange sauce, put the sugar and vinegar in a saucepan over high heat and stir until the sugar is dissolved. Keep stirring and bring the vinegar to the boil. Add the stock, orange juice and Madeira, stirring, and bring back to the boil. Add the bay leaf and reduce the heat so the sauce simmers gently and reduces by half. Add the butter and mix through until melted, then remove the pan from the heat and set aside until needed.

To serve, divide the celeriac mash evenly between four plates, then place two discs of the ballotine on top. Spoon some of the orange sauce over and around the plate and serve with some steamed spinach to the side.

Feeds 4

NOTE

To cook your duck sausage, preheat the oven to 220°C (415°F) (fan-forced 200°C/400°F). Heat some olive oil or butter in a frying pan and when hot add your sausage and cook turning and basting all the time. You want to render out the fat from the skin and brown it also. Once well browned put the sausage in a baking dish in the oven for about 15 minutes, basting every couple of minutes. Remove from the oven and rest for a few minutes, then slice and serve. Eat with the celeriac mash and steamed spinach or couscous and roast veggie salad on page 22, lentil, parsley and tomato salad on page 100 or even the bok choy stir-fry on page 112.

I am generally known for my love of cooking with beer, but every now and then I like to branch out and cook with other wonderful ingredients—in this case alcoholic apple cider. There has been an incredible explosion of handmade craft ciders in the market over the last few years, which make things exciting for cooking as well as drinking.

SLOW-COOKED LEG OF LAMB IN CIDER WITH OLIVES

1 deboned lamb leg (about 1.8 kg/4 lb), tied up
4 garlic cloves, 2 peeled and quartered lengthway,
   2 thinly sliced
salt and freshly ground black pepper
80 ml (2½ fl oz/⅓ cup) olive oil
1 onion, sliced
4 anchovy fillets
2 carrots, peeled and diced
2 celery stalks, diced

650 ml (22½ fl oz) alcoholic apple cider*
250 ml (9 fl oz/1 cup) beef stock
1 tin (400 g/14 oz) chopped tomatoes
rind and juice of 1 orange
90 g (3¼ oz/½ cup) each kalamata olives and green
   olives (I use Spanish queens with pip)
1 teaspoon thyme
250 g (9 oz) button mushrooms
250 g (9 oz) green beans

Preheat the oven to 170°C (325°F) (fan-forced 150°C/300°F).

Stab the lamb with a sharp knife eight times and insert 1 sliver of garlic into each slit, then season with salt and pepper. Heat 2 tablespoons of the olive oil in a large frying pan over high heat. Add the lamb and sear on all sides, then remove from the pan, put on a plate and cover to keep warm.

To the same pan in which you browned the meat, add the remaining olive oil and when hot add the onion, thinly sliced garlic and anchovies. Cook for several minutes over medium–high heat. Add the carrot and celery and cook for 5 minutes to seal and colour a little. Put the lamb back in the pan, along with any juices. Add the apple cider, beef stock, tomatoes, orange rind, orange juice and olives. Season with the thyme, and some salt and pepper then bring to the boil.

Cover the pan with a lid or foil, transfer to the oven and cook for about 1¼ hours. Add the mushrooms and beans, cover and cook for another 10 minutes, then uncover and cook for a further 15 minutes. The lamb is cooked when it has reached an internal temperature of around 60–62°C (140–144°F)

If there is still a lot of liquid in the pan, remove the lamb and vegetables and keep warm, put the roasting dish on the stovetop over medium–high heat and reduce the liquid down to a runny gravy consistency. Season the gravy with salt and pepper as needed, then return the vegetables to warm through.

Pour any juice from the lamb into the gravy and stir. Slice the lamb into thick slices (about 8 mm/⅜ in) and then serve 2–3 slices per person with the vegetables and gravy.

Feeds 6–8

NOTE

Use an alcoholic cider
that's around the
7 per cent alcohol level.

Traditionally, wellington is a beef dish wrapped in crêpes, then a mushroom duxelles, then some chicken pâté and then encased in pastry and baked. I decided to take a shortcut or two by making a duck liver and mushroom pâté and instead of crêpes I wrapped the loin in blanched silverbeet. There are a few steps in this recipe, but the end result is well worth it! You may want to hold this recipe in the wings for when you have a nice little dinner party planned for some close friends.

VENISON WELLINGTON ON POACHED BEETROOT WITH RED WINE SAUCE

1 venison loin or beef loin (about 1 kg/2 lb 4 oz)

salt and freshly ground black pepper

2 tablespoons olive oil

1 tablespoon butter

½ onion, finely diced

3 spring onions (scallions), thinly sliced

2 garlic cloves, finely chopped

1 teaspoon lemon thyme

300 g (10½ oz/3⅓ cups) roughly chopped Swiss brown mushrooms

350 g (12 oz) duck livers, cleaned of sinew

100 ml (3½ fl oz) Madeira, port or brandy

250 ml (9 fl oz/1 cup) cream

1 bunch silverbeet (Swiss chard)

1 sheet puff pastry

1 free-range egg, beaten

Poached Beetroot

2 large beetroot (beets)

about 250 ml (9 fl oz/1 cup) dry white wine (I used chardonnay)

juice of ½ lemon (about 1 tablespoon)

80 g (2¾ oz) unsalted butter

½ teaspoon lemon thyme

Red Wine Sauce

2 tablespoons butter

1 tablespoon very finely chopped spring onion (scallion)

125 ml (4 fl oz/½ cup) red wine (I used shiraz)

125 ml (4 fl oz/½ cup) beef stock

1 teaspoon freshly ground black pepper

1 tablespoon balsamic vinegar

1 teaspoon dijon mustard

pinch of white sugar

Preheat the oven to 220°C (415°F) (fan-forced 200°C/400°F).

Clean any fat or sinew off the loin and season well. Heat 1 tablespoon of the olive oil in a frying pan over high heat. When the oil is smoking carefully add the loin and brown well on all sides. When the meat is well browned all over and caramelised, remove from the hot pan onto a plate and leave to cool.

In the same pan you used to brown the venison, heat the remaining olive oil and the butter over medium–high heat. Add the onion and spring onion and cook for several minutes, then add the garlic and lemon thyme and cook for another 5 minutes or so. Add the mushrooms and a pinch of salt, then cook down for about 10 minutes, stirring every now and then. Add the duck livers and cook for a couple of minutes—you want the livers to be medium-rare. Add the Madeira and flame the pan, giving everything a good stir. Add the cream and season with salt and black pepper. Turn the heat down and simmer for a couple more minutes. Put the pâté mixture into a blender and pulse until it is a rough paste—it should be a firm paste. Set aside to cool.

Wash the silverbeet well, then cut the leaves away from the white stems and discard the stems. Blanch the leaves in boiling salted water for about 30 seconds, then put in a bowl of iced water for 5 minutes to refresh. Remove the leaves and dry with paper towel—you should have some nice large soft silverbeet leaves.

Place a piece of baking paper on a baking tray and then place the sheet of puff pastry on top of that. Cover the pastry with half of the silverbeet leaves, making sure to leave all four sides of the pastry clear. Now spread some of the pâté over the leaves, about 1 cm (½ in) thick. Place the venison loin on top of the pâté and spread a layer of pâté on top of the venison and around the sides and end. Finish off by using the remaining silverbeet leaves to cover the top and sides of the loin. Next, depending on how big the pastry sheet is, wrap one side up and over the venison and then wash the top of it with the beaten egg. Wrap the other side up and over so that it overlaps the first side. If the two sides don't actually meet up, wrap them up and over as far as possible and then brush with the egg wash and cut another piece of pastry (rectangle size) and lay that over the top so that it covers the gap and drapes over the two sides. Seal each end, cut away any excess pastry and use a fork to decorate and crimp the pastry closed. Put the wellington in the oven and bake for about 25 minutes until the pastry is golden brown and crispy. Rest for ten minutes before carving.

Meanwhile, poach the beetroot and prepare the sauce.

Cut three 5 mm (¼ in) thick rounds from each beetroot—don't throw the rest out, use in a fresh juice or salad. In a large frying pan over medium–high heat add enough white wine to just cover the beetroot slices, then add the lemon juice, butter and lemon thyme and bring to the boil. Reduce the heat to a simmer and cover. Cook until the beetroot is just tender but still has a little bite in the middle. Drain the beetroot, then put on a plate, covered, and keep warm.

In a small saucepan over medium–high heat put 1 tablespoon of the butter and when foaming add the spring onion and cook for several minutes. Add the wine, stock and pepper and bring to the boil, then turn down to a strong simmer and reduce by two-thirds. Add the balsamic and mustard and stir to combine, taste and add the sugar accordingly. Add the remaining butter and combine. The sauce should be glossy and syrupy. Strain through a fine-mesh sieve to remove any cracked pepper and return to the pan to keep warm.

To serve, place a piece of the poached beetroot in the middle of a dinner plate. Cut a 3 cm (1¼ in) thick piece from the wellington and stand that up on the beetroot slice—don't lay it down. Drizzle the red wine sauce around the plate and eat!

Serve this with a side of steamed halved brussels sprouts or some steamed asparagus and a side of roasted potatoes.

Feeds 6

The great thing about this dish is its simplicity and of course the reliance on the fruit of the season. You could do this with a mix of summer berries or tropical fruit like mangoes, nectarines and lychees or make it with several varieties of plums or make an apricot and pear tart. Whatever looks good and is in season will work and it will taste fantastic.

APPLE, PEACH AND HAZELNUT TART

3 white or yellow peaches (or both)
2 apples (such as golden delicious, granny smith, pink lady or even a mix)
45 g (1⅔ oz/¼ cup lightly packed) soft brown sugar
80 ml (2½ fl oz/⅓ cup) calvados
2 tablespoons unsalted butter
130 g (4⅔ oz) hazelnuts, skin removed

55 g (1¾ oz/¼ cup) caster (superfine) sugar
grated zest of 1 lemon
¼ teaspoon ground cinnamon
½ teaspoon natural vanilla extract
1 free-range egg, plus 1 extra for brushing the pastry
1 puff pastry sheet

Preheat the oven to 200°C (400°F) (fan-forced 180°C/350°F).

Put the peaches in boiling water for 30 seconds then remove and refresh in cold water, peel, halve, remove the stones and cut into slices. Peel the apples, core and cut into thin slices, then put in a bowl with the peach. Add the brown sugar and 2 tablespoons of the calvados and mix it all to combine.

Melt half the butter in a frying pan over medium heat, tip in the fruit and any juices and fry for about 5 minutes, stirring and tossing all the time. Remove from the heat and set aside to cool.

Put the hazelnuts in a food processor and blend with the caster sugar, then add the lemon zest, cinnamon, remaining calvados, vanilla, remaining butter and the egg. Blend into a smooth paste.

Lay a piece of baking paper on a baking tray and place the puff pastry on top. Spread the nut mixture over the puff pastry but leave a 2 cm (¾ in) gap around the edges. Lay the cooled fruit over the hazelnut mixture—in alternating apple and peach slices if you like—and drizzle over all the juice. The fruit can be warm but make sure it is not hot or it will melt the nut mixture.

Using your thumb and forefinger of both hands go around the sides of the pastry pinching and lifting the pastry up and over slightly, folding over the piece next to it to resemble a rustic looking plait. Brush the pastry with the beaten egg. Bake in the centre of your oven for 25–30 minutes until golden brown and the plaited sides have risen. Remove from the oven and cool just enough so you can hold a piece to your lips and bite into it!

Serve with ice cream.

Feeds 6–8

Just in case you are wondering and you probably are, a clafoutis (pronounced 'kla-FOO-tee') is a rustic French baked dessert made by baking cherries in a custard-like batter similar to pancake batter. Just in case you are still wondering, that is the traditional French spelling! This is a perfect dish to be cooking when cherries are in season and a great dessert for a dinner party.

MORELLO CHERRY CLAFOUTIS

35 g (1¼ oz/¼ cup) self-raising flour
110 g (3¾ oz/½ cup firmly packed) brown sugar
pinch of salt
25 g (1 oz/¼ cup) almond meal
4 free-range eggs
2 free-range egg yolks
450 ml (16 fl oz) milk

150 ml (5 fl oz) pouring cream
2 tablespoons port
50 g (1¾ oz) butter, melted, plus extra for greasing
600 g (1 lb 5 oz) pitted cherries or morello cherries*
grated zest of 1 lemon
grated zest of 1 orange

Preheat the oven to 190°C (375°F) (fan-forced 170°C/325°F).

Sift the flour, sugar and salt together into a bowl, then mix through the almond meal. In a separate bowl, whisk the eggs, egg yolks, milk, cream and port together. Gradually incorporate the flour mixture into the milk mixture, whisking all the time, until you finally have a smooth liquid batter. Set aside.

Grease an ovenproof casserole dish with butter and then scatter the pitted cherries around the dish—the bottom should be completely covered. Next, whisk the melted butter and the lemon and orange zests into the batter and carefully pour the mixture over the cherries.

Place the dish in the oven and cook for about 50 minutes until browned on top and firmish to touch. Leave to stand for a few minutes—the clafoutis should wobble in a firm way—then serve with ice cream, yoghurt or cream.

Feeds 8

NOTE: If you use morello cherries, they're quite large, which I like, so you can afford to cut them in half to remove the seed. You could also make this dish using morello cherries from a jar but you may need to up the sugar to counter the sourness from the jarred variety.

》》》》》》》》》》》》》》》》》》》》
TIP
There are various ways to remove the seed from a cherry— perhaps the most straightforward is to cut it in half and then use your knife to pry out the pit. You can buy pitters at kitchen stores which will do the job and also keep the cherries whole.
》》》》》》》》》》》》》》》》》》》》

CHAPTER 5

The one THAT DIDN'T get away

*O*kay, I have a confession to make—cooking seafood scares me! Some people seem to be really good at it without even trying, others, me included, seem to have to work harder at it. I know people who are brilliant at cooking seafood but can't cook anything else, including toast for their own breakfast! It doesn't make sense, but then there are lots of things in life that don't make sense. That said, the sensible thing to do when starting out cooking a seafood dish is to get the best quality seafood you can find—that goes for all the ingredients really. If you start with a tired old piece of fish and some wilted snow peas then the dish is not going to get any better after 35 minutes of cooking! The next bit of advice is don't take shortcuts— don't try and cook it a bit quicker and don't overcook it (I learnt all these things the hard way)—just let the seafood cook itself, so to speak. If you follow my recipes, keep an eye on things and taste as you go you'll be cooking like a seafood pro in no time.

Some people would say there is only one way to serve oysters and that is *au naturel*. I must confess, though, that while I do love a beautiful fresh oyster my limit is probably about three before I head for the bacon and worcestershire sauce. In my first cookbook, *Mercurio's Menu*, I did oysters three ways, all of them delicious of course, but as they say there is more than one way to skin a cat so here, for your eating pleasure, are another two ways to eat an oyster.

OYSTERS TWO WAYS

Stout Mornay Oysters
2 teaspoons butter
2 teaspoons plain (all-purpose) flour
60 ml (4 fl oz/¼ cup) milk
60 ml (4 fl oz/¼ cup) stout
25 g (1 oz/¼ cup) grated cheddar cheese
25 g (1 oz/¼ cup) freshly grated parmesan cheese
salt and freshly ground black pepper

Soy and Sake Oysters
1 tablespoon soy sauce
2 tablespoons sake
grated zest of 1 lemon
2 tablespoons roughly crushed wasabi peas

1 dozen of the freshest oysters you can get

Preheat oven grill (broiler) to high.

To make the stout mornay sauce, first make a roux by heating the butter in a saucepan over medium heat until it begins to foam, then gradually add the flour, stirring well as you do. Let this mixture cook for a few minutes, continuing to stir— this will cook the flour taste out of it. Make sure you do not colour the roux by cooking it over too high a heat. Next, slowly whisk in the milk so that it combines well with the roux, then gradually whisk in the stout. If the sauce is too thick and you need to add more liquid, add in equal amounts of beer and milk. You want the sauce to have a consistency a bit like thick pouring custard and keep in mind that when you add the cheeses the sauce will thicken a little more. When you are happy with the consistency of the sauce, add the cheeses and mix through so that they melt into the sauce, then season with salt and pepper as needed.

Using half the oysters, spoon some of the mixture over each oyster, making sure they are completely covered so the oyster steams itself inside the mornay mix. Place under the grill and cook until the tops are nicely browned.

To make the soy and sake sauce, mix the soy and sake together and spoon over the remaining half a dozen oysters. Place a generous pinch of lemon zest on each oyster and then a pinch of the crushed wasabi peas.

Eat and enjoy.

These mini recipes are each enough for six oysters, so if serving a dozen of each just double the mixtures.

> »»»»»»»»»»»»»»»»»»
> **TIP**
> Put the peas on just before eating the soy and sake oysters or else they will soak up the soy and sake dressing and become soft. The wasabi peas offer a textural crunch that complements the softness of the oyster and also add a little bit of that Japanese heat that complements the soy.
> »»»»»»»»»»»»»»»»»»

 181

I made this dish as part of a chef's challenge on a TV show—the challenge was 'best eggs benedict'. My plan was to make a great benedict, but with a difference, and it didn't work! I lost to a very straight and narrow traditional version, not because it was necessarily better, but because mine was too different. I tell you though, if you give this recipe a go you will give me a ten out of ten.

EGGS BENEDICT WITH BLUE SWIMMER CRAB

Potato Rosti
2 waxy potatoes (such as desiree), grated
½ teaspoon plain (all-purpose) flour
1 free-range egg, beaten
olive oil, for shallow-frying

Hollandaise de la Beer
60 ml (2 fl oz/¼ cup) white wine vinegar
60 ml (2 fl oz/¼ cup) lambic (fruit) beer*
pinch of white pepper
3 free-range egg yolks
200 g (7 oz) unsalted butter, melted
freshly ground black pepper (optional)

Asparagus
1 bunch asparagus (I like to use thin or baby
    asparagus as they are more delicate)

Blue Swimmer Crab
1 tablespoon unsalted butter
200 g (7 oz) blue swimmer crab*
2 tablespoons chopped tarragon

Perfect Poached Eggs
1 tablespoon white wine vinegar
2 super-fresh free-range eggs (I use eggs from an
    800 g/1 lb 12 oz carton)

To make the rosti, squeeze as much liquid out of the grated potato as you can—I squeeze it out with my hands and then lay the potato between sheets of paper towel and press down firmly—and then put the grated potato in a bowl. Sprinkle in the flour and about a quarter of the beaten egg and mix well. (You don't want to create a wet mix, you just want the potato to hold together.)

Pour some olive oil into a frying pan, about 1 cm (½ in) deep, then heat over medium–high heat until you can see it shimmering. Take half the potato mix, form it into a ball or patty shape, and then repeat with the remaining mix to make a second patty. Carefully put the patties into the pan and use an egg slide to flatten and spread them out—the patties should be about 8 mm (⅜ in) thick. When golden brown on one side gently flip and cook until golden brown on the other. Remove from the pan and transfer onto paper towel to drain. Season with a little salt. Keep warm in a low oven until needed.

To make the hollandaise de la beer, put the vinegar, beer and white pepper in a small saucepan over medium–high heat and bring to the boil. Cook until it has reduced by two-thirds. Remove from the stove and leave to cool.

Take a medium-sized saucepan and add cold water until it is a quarter full. Bring the water to the boil, then turn the heat down so that the water is barely simmering (and when I say barely I mean hardly simmering at all). Take a glass bowl that will fit snugly on top of the pan but won't come in contact with the water and place it on top of the pan. Put the egg yolks and the vinegar and beer reduction in the bowl and beat together using a whisk. Continue to beat for about 4 minutes. The mixture will double in size and thicken into a pale foamy sauce—this is known as a sabayon. Continue to whisk and gradually add the melted butter. Once all the butter has been added you should have a thick, creamy and buttery sauce. Taste for seasoning and add some black pepper if you want. Set the hollandaise aside in a warm place and leave the hot water on the stove.

To prepare the asparagus, break the woody ends off and discard. Drop the asparagus into the pan with the hot water that you used to steam the hollandaise. Leave for about 2–3 minutes or until they are tender but still have some bite. Remove and rinse with cold water to stop the cooking process, but do not let them get cold, then set aside.

To prepare the crab, heat the butter in a fr ying pan over medium heat and when melted add the crab and stir so that it breaks up and cooks for 3 minutes. Add the chopped tarragon and mix through. Be careful not to overcook the crab as it may toughen. Set aside until needed.

If you really want perfect poached eggs then you have to start with the freshest free-range eggs you can find. When eggs are super-fresh the white remain beautiful and tight when they cook. If your eggs are old then the whites will run and be thin and wispy. Fresh is best!

Take a good size saucepan and fill it with water so that it is about three times the depth of the egg (before breaking in). Add the vinegar and heat over high heat until the water comes to a simmer, then reduce the heat so the water barely moves. I use a thermometer and hold the water at about 80°C (175°F). Break the eggs into separate small bowls—this will make them easier to put in the water. Carefully drop each egg into the pan and cook gently until just set—remember they will continue to cook when you remove them so take them out when you think they are not quite ready.

While the eggs are poaching, get two plates out (sometimes I put my plates in a warm oven so they are not stone cold when I serve this dish, especially if I'm serving it to someone special as breakfast in bed!), place one rosti on each plate, then divide the asparagus equally and neatly on top of each rosti. Next, spoon the crab meat on top of the asparagus so it is a uniform layer and then make a little indent in the middle of the crab meat—this leaves a place for the poached egg to sit. Remove the eggs from the pan using a slotted spoon and place on top of the crab, then generously spoon over the beer hollandaise. Lastly, season with some pepper and serve.

Feeds 2

NOTES

The fruit beer I use for this is Timmermans Framboise from Belgium, made with raspberries—it can be a little hard to find but worth the effort.

You can buy beautiful fresh picked frozen blue swimmer crab from your local fishmonger. It comes frozen usually in 500 g (1 lb 2 oz) packets so all you need to do is cut the portion you want off the frozen block and put the rest back in the freezer for next time.

If you want to make this for four people double the potato quantity and use two bunches of asparagus. You should have enough hollandaise for four serves and you will have enough crab if you bought a 500 g (1 lb 2 oz) packet and only need 100 g (3½ oz) per person.

This is a different way of curing and eating salmon—drawing some of the moisture out to firm the fillets up so they become meaty, changing the texture and flavour. If you left the salmon in this cure for two days you would end up with gravlax. You can add other things to the cure to flavour it such as lemon or orange zest and herbs, but I really just want to accentuate the meat character and then pair that with the wasabi mayo.

SALT, SUGAR AND HONEY-CURED SALMON WITH WASABI MAYO

130 g (4⅔ oz/1 cup) sea salt
220 g (7¾ oz/1 cup) white sugar
4 tail-end salmon fillets, skin off (about 200 g/
    7 oz each)

175 g (6 oz/½ cup) honey
2 tablespoons olive oil
120 g (4¼ oz/½ cup) whole-egg mayonnaise
2 tablespoons wasabi paste*

Crush the salt and sugar using a mortar and pestle and then spread half the mixture out evenly in a dish that will fit the salmon. Wash and dry the salmon fillets and then place onto the sugar salt cure. Cover the top of the salmon with the rest of the salt mixture and press down to coat well. Drizzle over the honey, then cover the dish with plastic wrap and refrigerate for a couple of hours.

Remove the salmon from the fridge and turn the fillets over. Cover again with plastic wrap, put back in the fridge and leave for another 2 hours. You will notice a lot of liquid has come out of the fillets and this is what you want. You are drawing out the water and in its place the fish is taking in the sugar, salt and honey flavours.

Remove the fish from the cure and rinse under cold running water—the fillets should have firmed up due to the curing process. Dry the fillets well.

Heat the olive oil in a large frying pan over medium–high heat. Add the fillets (if the pan is not big enough you can cook in two batches and just keep the first batch warm in a low oven) and sear on both sides until nicely browned—you will get some caramelisation thanks to the honey. Be careful not to overcook as the fish is already cured, so you can leave it rare in the middle—if you overcook it, it will become very dry. Remove the fillets and place on a plate until everything is ready to serve.

To make the wasabi mayo mix the mayonnaise with a generous squeeze of wasabi paste—adjust the heat to your liking by adding more wasabi, but remember you can't take the wasabi out if you add too much! If you do over-wasabi it you can add more mayo to dilute the heat.

I like to serve this with my bok choy stir-fry (see page 112). Put the bok choy into the middle of the plate, drape a fillet over half of the bok choy then dollop a generous spoonful or two of the wasabi mayo over the salmon and eat!

Feeds 4

NOTE

You can find tubes of wasabi paste wasabi paste in the Asian aisle at your supermarket.

The key to this salad and really to anything you cook is absolute freshness! If everything in this salad is as fresh as can be then the flavours will zing out in absolute harmony and the contrast in texture, sweetness and clarity will certainly bring a smile to your face as you're eating. I like to make the dressing first so it has some time to sit, allowing the flavours to combine.

SEAFOOD SALAD

2 small calamari tubes or 1 large one
1 tablespoon unsalted butter
1 garlic clove, crushed
1 red bird's-eye chilli, thinly sliced
20 raw prawns (shrimp), peeled and deveined, tails left intact
12 scallops
100 g (3½ oz) enoki mushrooms, bottom part of the stems cut off and discarded
1 red capsicum (pepper), julienned
1 Lebanese (short) cucumber, peeled, seeded and julienned
1 carrot, julienned
1 small red onion, halved and very thinly sliced
3 tablespoon chopped coriander (cilantro) leaves
10 mint leaves, roughly chopped
1 butter lettuce or mignonette lettuce leaves, washed

Dressing
1 tablespoon olive oil
1 tablespoon white wine vinegar
2 tablespoons lime juice
2 tablespoons soy sauce
2 teaspoons caster (superfine) sugar
2 teaspoons sesame oil
½ teaspoon fish sauce
½ teaspoon garlic powder
¼ teaspoon chilli powder

If you have small calamari tubes give them a wash and then thinly slice them into small rings. If you have one large tube, cut it open like a book, remove any cartilage, wash, then cut in half. Use a sharp knife and finely score the inside or soft side of the two pieces in a crisscross pattern, then cut into 4 x 1 cm (1½ x ½ in) strips.

To make the dressing, combine all the ingredients in a jar, put the lid on and give it a really good shake. You want a really fine balance between the sourness from the lime, sweetness from the sugar, saltiness from the soy and the pungency from the fish sauce. Adjust in very small amounts if necessary.

Melt the butter in a frying pan over medium heat, then add the garlic and chilli and gently fry for a couple of minutes. Turn the heat up to medium–high, add the prawns and scallops and cook for 2–3 minutes, stirring so they turn and get colour on both sides. Add the calamari and cook for another 2 minutes, tossing so they cook evenly. When the prawns are just cooked, remove everything from the pan, put in a bowl and set aside while you finish the salad.

Put all of the remaining salad ingredients into a large bowl, giving them a good toss to combine evenly. Add the warm prawns, scallops and calamari and mix through, then add the dressing and mix again. Divide everything evenly between four plates or bowls and enjoy with a nice glass of wine!

Feeds 4

This recipe was my first attempt at following the food trend of 'stacking' or creating height on the plate. I have to say it worked out terrifically, backed up by the fact that it not only looked good but tasted great as well. You can buy a stacking ring from a kitchen shop or you can just borrow a bit of PVC piping from your plumber—either will work fine. Make sure you pack the ingredients down with some firmness so they settle and you can remove the ring without the stack collapsing. This recipe is for two as I think it suits a more romantic environment, however, it is easily doubled up to feed four.

MEDITERRANEAN LOBSTER STACK WITH HERB VINAIGRETTE

1 eggplant (aubergine)
2 tablespoons olive oil, plus extra if needed
1 large red capsicum (pepper), with four squarish
    sides as you will need four cheeks for this
    recipe
1 tin (400 g/14 oz) chickpeas, drained and rinsed
1 lobster tail (about 350–400 g/12–14 oz), cut in half
    lengthways
1 tablespoon unsalted butter
1 tablespoon finely chopped tarragon

1 radicchio lettuce
salt and freshly ground black pepper

Vinaigrette
80 ml (2½ fl oz/⅓ cup) olive oil
2 tablespoons red wine vinegar
2 tablespoons lemon juice
1 tablespoon each finely chopped tarragon,
    chervil, chives and flat-leaf (Italian) parsley
1 teaspoon dijon mustard

Slice four 3 mm (⅛ in) rounds from thickest part of the eggplant. Heat the olive oil in a frying pan over medium–high heat. Add the eggplant rings and fry for 5–10 minutes or until cooked—the eggplant should be lovely and soft and golden brown on both sides—you may need to add another tablespoon or two of olive oil when you turn the eggplants over. Remove from the pan and set aside on paper towel.

Preheat your grill (broiler) to high.

Slice the sides off the capsicum and put them, skin side up, under the grill. Cook until the skin blackens all over. Place the blackened capsicum in a plastic bag to sweat for several minutes. Remove the capsicum pieces from the bag, one at a time, and peel off and discard the skin. Place the peeled capsicum on a plate and set aside.

Place the chickpeas in a bowl and lightly squash them so they won't roll around on the plates but still retain their individual shape.

To easily remove the lobster meat from the shell, dip each half into some boiling water for about 10–15 seconds then remove. Use a dessertspoon to scoop the meat away from the shell and chop into bite-sized pieces.

Put the butter and tarragon in a frying pan over medium heat and cook until the butter begins to foam. Add the lobster meat and cook gently for several minutes. Season the lobster with a little salt and black pepper, add four radicchio leaves to the pan and continue to cook until the radicchio has wilted. Remove the pan from the heat and set aside.

To make the vinaigrette, put the olive oil, vinegar, lemon juice, chopped herbs, mustard, and some salt and black pepper in a jar, put the lid on and give it a really good shake. Pour 2 teaspoons of the vinaigrette over the squashed chickpeas and mix in. Set the rest aside.

To serve, put an 8 cm (3¼ in) diameter stacking ring (or PVC piping) in the centre of a large flat plate. Stack the ingredients in the following order, making sure to push each layer down firmly:

1 wilted radicchio leaf
2 tablespoons chickpeas
1 eggplant ring (trim to fit if needed)
2 tablespoons lobster meat
1 piece of capsicum (trim to fit if needed)
2 tablespoons chickpeas
2 tablespoons lobster meat
1 radicchio leaf
1 eggplant ring
1 piece of capsicum

Press down gently to firm up the stack and then carefully remove the stacking ring. Repeat with the other plate. Drizzle the vinaigrette over and around the stack and serve with some crusty bread and a glass of good sav blanc white.

Feeds 2

This is a pretty simple dish to make that is bursting with flavours and is also a little different! You can buy pickled octopus in jars or by the spoonful at your local gourmet deli or supermarket. I love to eat the octopus on its own—well, with a beer—but in this salad it is equally delicious. I love the octopus' texture and how it contrasts with the crunch of the fennel, and the bitterness from the radicchio is tempered by the vinegar from the pickling character. It is quite a light salad which I think is ideal as a lunch treat or an entrée.

OCTOPUS SALAD WITH HUMMUS AND ROASTED TOMATOES

16 cherry tomatoes, halved
salt
80 ml (2½ fl oz/⅓ cup) olive oil
2 tablespoons balsamic vinegar
1 teaspoon wholegrain mustard
freshly ground black pepper
200–250 g (7–9 oz) hummus (to make your own,
   see page 56)

1 fennel bulb, thinly sliced
1 radicchio lettuce, four leaves per serve, torn into
   three pieces each
200–250 g (7–9 oz) pickled octopus, thinly sliced
   reserving any tentacles for garnish
45 g (1⅔ oz/1 cup) baby rocket (arugula) leaves

Preheat the oven to 180°C (350°F) (fan-forced 160°C/315°F).

Put the tomatoes in a bowl, sprinkle with salt and add 2 tablespoons of the olive oil, then mix to coat well. Place the tomatoes on a baking tray and roast until they just start to break down. Remove from the oven and set aside.

Whisk the remaining oil, vinegar and mustard together in a bowl, season with salt and pepper, and then set aside.

Lay out four plates or wide-rimmed bowls. Place 2–3 tablespoons of hummus in the middle of each plate or bowl. Place the fennel and radicchio around the hummus. Place a pile of octopus on top of the hummus and garnish with a tentacle or two. Toss the baby rocket through the vinaigrette and then tower on top of the octopus. Scatter the tomatoes over and around the plate, then drizzle vinaigrette over so it soaks down to the fennel and serve.

Feeds 4

This is one of those dishes that is easy to cook, but hard to describe, so you will have to have a go and see what works for you. What I mean is you may find exquisite baby squid to use, in which case you may have three or four per person because they are so small and delicate and you could serve them whole. Or you may have to use large squid and cut them and truss them. Cooking is like that, which is what I love about it, sometimes you have to use what there is rather than what you want—the good thing about that is it keeps you creative and inventive.

SQUID STUFFED WITH CRAB MEAT AND MANGO SALSA

2 tablespoons unsalted butter

500 g (1 lb 2 oz) crab meat

generous pinch of salt, plus ½ teaspoon extra

¼ teaspoon white pepper

2 tablespoons finely chopped tarragon

4 small squid tubes (about 12–14 cm/4½–5½ in) long or 2 large ones

2 tablespoons rice flour

2 tablespoons plain (all-purpose) flour

½ teaspoon freshly ground black pepper

2 tablespoons paprika

2 tablespoons peanut oil

Mango Salsa

2 tablespoons butter

1 long red chilli, thinly sliced

2 tablespoons very finely diced red capsicum (pepper)

2 tablespoons finely chopped chives

2 ripe but firm mangoes, flesh cut away and diced

1 teaspoon curry powder

125 ml (4 fl oz/½ cup) coconut milk

80 g (2¾ oz/½ cup) pine nuts

180 g (6¼ oz/4 cups) baby English spinach leaves

Heat the butter in a frying pan over medium–high heat. Add the crab meat and cook, stirring for a couple of minutes, then add the pinch of salt, white pepper and tarragon and continue to cook and stir for another couple of minutes until the crab is just cooked. Remove from the heat and set aside to cool a little.

You can buy squid whole and clean it yourself or you can ask your fishmonger to clean them for you, which is easier. Give the squid a wash under cold water and just check that there isn't any cartilage left in the tubes, then dry it well. Gently stuff the squid with the crab mixture, being careful not to split the squid by forcing too much meat inside or filling it too tightly. You can fill them up but you don't need to jam the meat in.

If using two large squid tubes, cut the squid tube on one side so that you can open it out into a square or rectangle. Make sure any cartilage is removed and the inside is clean. Score the soft inside flesh quite deeply in two directions so that you get lots of little squares or diamonds. Turn the squid over so that the scored side is on your work surface. Place a generous amount of the crab meat along ▶▶▶

The sensible thing to do when starting out cooking a seafood dish is get the best quality seafood you can find. The next bit of advice is don't take shortcuts ... let the seafood cook itself.

←◂◂

the middle of the squid, running lengthways, and then lift the side closest to you and the opposite side up so they meet. Take a long wooden skewer and starting from the right (unless you are left handed in which case I presume you will start from the left) thread it through the squid to weave from the front flap to the back flap and then through the back flap into the front flap, sealing the lip closed. Once closed you can push a little more crab meat into either end to stuff it a little tighter, but be careful not to split the squid from the skewer. It should look like a weird looking curly sausage. Repeat with the remaining squid tube.

Combine the rice flour and plain flour on a plate and season with the ½ teaspoon salt, black pepper and paprika and mix well to combine. Roll the stuffed squid over the flour to evenly coat, then dust off any excess. Heat the peanut oil in a frying pan over high heat. Add the squid and cook, turning often so that all sides cook and brown evenly. Remove from the pan and set aside, covered, to keep warm.

To make the mango salsa, heat half the butter in a frying pan and when it begins to foam add the chilli, capsicum and chives. Cook for a few minutes, then add the mango and give it a good stir. Sprinkle over the curry powder, mix through and cook for a little longer, then add the coconut milk to give the salsa a little bit of moisture. Remove from the heat.

Put the pine nuts in a small dry frying pan over medium–high heat and toast until slightly coloured, then remove and set aside. To the same pan, add the remaining butter and when foaming add the spinach. Stir through and cook until the spinach has wilted. Remove from the heat and toss through the pine nuts.

To serve, evenly divide the wilted spinach and pine nuts between four plates, cut each squid into three pieces and arrange on top of the spinach then spoon some salsa to the side of the squid. If you ended up using two large squid tubes then cut each one in half and then each half in half again and serve two pieces to each plate.

Feeds 4

I am lucky enough to live four minutes away from Port Phillip Bay which just happens to have several mussel farms I can see from the shore. On Sundays I go down to the jetty and buy a kilo of mussels that have been freshly plucked from the ocean that morning, and by that evening they are swimming in a delicious broth being enthusiastically slurped up by yours truly. Fantastic! There are several companies now vacuum-packing live cleaned mussels in one kilo bags which is a perfect size for a dinner for two. All you need to do is cut the bag open and tip the contents into a pot and away you go.

MUSSEL SOUP

2 kg (4 lb 8 oz) blue mussels
4 tablespoons unsalted butter
3 garlic cloves, finely chopped
3 red bird's-eye chilli, thinly sliced
2 tablespoons chopped flat-leaf (Italian) parsley, plus 10 g (¼ oz/⅓ cup) extra
250 ml (9 fl oz/1 cup) dry white wine

1 tablespoon olive oil
2 leeks, white part only, finely chopped
2 tins (800 g/1 lb 12 oz in total) diced tomatoes
freshly ground black pepper
10 g (¼ oz/⅓ cup) chopped basil
4 pieces lemon rind, finely sliced

Scrub and debeard the mussels, discard any with broken shells and set the rest aside in a colander.

Melt half the butter in a big saucepan over medium–high heat. Add half the garlic and half the chilli and gently fry until aromatic, being careful not to burn them, then add the 2 tablespoons of parsley and cook for another 2 minutes. Increase the heat to high and add the mussels and 125 ml (4 fl oz/½ cup) of the wine. Put the lid on and cook for several minutes, shaking the pan to encourage the mussels to open. Once you see steam forcing itself out from under the lid, remove the lid and check if all or most of the mussels are open. If so, remove from the heat, pour the contents of the pan into a colander sitting over a bowl to catch all the cooking liquor. Set aside.

Using the same pan, heat the remaining butter and the olive oil over medium heat. Add the leek and cook gently for 5 minutes, then add the remaining garlic and chilli and gently cook until the garlic is translucent—about 2–3 minutes. Turn the heat to high, add the remaining wine and the tomatoes, stir through to combine then strain the mussel cooking liquor through a fine-mesh sieve into the pan. Season with lots of pepper and bring to the boil. Reduce the heat and simmer for 20 minutes. Add the extra parsley, the basil and lemon zest and allow the flavours to blend for about 5–8 minutes, then add the mussels and mix through so they get all the broth through them and cook for 1–2 minutes to heat the mussels through.

Divide between four big deep bowls and serve with some freshly baked crusty bread and a spoon to slurp up the fantastic broth.

Feeds 4

》》》》》》》》》》》》》》》》》》》》》
TIP
Don't throw out any mussels that haven't opened—if you bought the mussels really fresh they are probably okay, just pry them open with a knife and if they smell okay, eat them.
》》》》》》》》》》》》》》》》》》》》》

Chowder is one of those dishes that everyone gets excited about, but no one really makes, instead leaving it to the local café or gastro pub to serve it up. Well, I say bugger that, get up off the couch, go shopping and get the ingredients and then make this recipe—you'll be happy you did and so will your family and friends. It freezes well, too, which is always a bonus when you find some while cleaning out your freezer—lunch!

SMOKED FISH CHOWDER

4 corn cobs
2 tablespoons unsalted butter
1 tablespoon olive oil
1 leek, white part only, diced
80 g (2¾ oz) speck, bacon or pancetta, diced
2 garlic cloves, chopped
2 celeriac, peeled and diced into 2 cm (¾ in) cubes
1 cauliflower head, pulled apart into florets
300 g (10½ fl oz) cold smoked kipper fillets, skin on, roughly chopped

1.5 litres (52 fl oz/6 cups) fish or chicken stock
330 ml (11¼ fl oz/1⅓ cups) pouring cream
½ teaspoon freshly ground black pepper
300 g (10½ oz) hot smoked mackerel, skin removed, broken into chunks
Tabasco sauce or another vinegar-based hot chilli sauce
2 tablespoons chopped dill
2 cheeks red capsicum (pepper), very finely diced

Rub the corn with half the butter, then grill them over the flame on your barbecue, stove or under the grill (broiler) until slightly blackened all over. Use a sharp knife to cut the kernels off the cobs, reserve the kernels and throw away the cobs.

Heat the remaining butter and the olive oil in a large saucepan over medium–high heat. Add the leek and speck and cook for several minutes, then add the garlic and cook for another 5 minutes. Add the corn kernels, celeriac and cauliflower and stir well to coat with the oil and leeks. Add the kipper fillets and stir through—there are tiny bones in the kipper fillets, but once the soup is cooked and blended they are not a problem. Add the stock and the cream and bring to the boil, then reduce the heat, season with pepper, and simmer for 20–30 minutes until the chowder is thick and the celeriac is cooked but not mushy. You will not need to season this dish with salt as the smoked fish adds quite a bit of saltiness, as does the stock.

Remove the pan from the heat and use a hand-held blender to blend the chowder well (or blend in a blender and then return to the pan). This is a chunky-style chowder, almost like a porridge rather than a soup. With the pan still on the heat add the mackerel and stir through, then add the Tabasco at your discretion—you want just a touch of heat for a background flavour. Taste for seasoning and adjust as needed. Stir through the chopped dill and serve in big bowls. Put a pinch of the finely diced red capsicum in the centre of the chowder and enjoy.

You could also serve the dish without the Tabasco and let those eating it add it at their discretion.

Feeds 8

NOTE

You can buy smoked fish from your local fishmonger or specialist delicatessen and the great thing is there are more boutique producers smoking their own style of fish than ever before.

This is a great dinner-party dish as it is simple to cook with the wow factor of gorgeous fresh lobster—who doesn't like that? The wow factor isn't just the lobster though, it's the combination of flavours and textures from the other ingredients, too. I love this sort of cooking where you take a hero ingredient and elevate it with a wonderful supporting cast of ingredients. The finished dish is more than just the story of the lobster; it is a love story between the chef, the ingredients and the diners.

LOBSTER LINGUINE

1 raw lobster tail (about 400 g/14 oz), halved lengthways
4 tablespoons butter
1 tablespoon olive oil
1 garlic clove, finely chopped
½ long red chilli, seeded and finely diced
pinch of salt
2 tablespoons finely chopped tarragon, plus extra to garnish
3 tablespoons finely chopped coriander (cilantro), plus extra to garnish

500 g (1 lb 2 oz) linguine
375 ml (13 fl oz /1½ cups) prosecco (or another sparkling wine or Champagne)
250 ml (9 fl oz/1 cup) fish or chicken stock
½ red onion, very finely diced
1 Thai red chilli or red bird's-eye chilli, very finely diced
1 zucchini (courgette), finely diced
1 tin (400 g/14 oz) borlotti beans or black-eyed peas, drained and rinsed
1 large tomato, peeled, seeded and finely diced

To easily remove the lobster meat from the shell, dip each half tail into some boiling water for about 10–15 seconds then remove. Use a dessertspoon to scoop the meat away from the shell and chop into bite-sized pieces.

Heat 1 tablespoon of the butter and the olive oil in a frying pan over medium heat, add the garlic and chilli and cook gently for a couple of minutes. Add the lobster and coat with the garlic and butter. Add a pinch of salt, 1 tablespoon each of the tarragon and coriander and combine. Cook for a couple of minutes until the lobster is just cooked, then remove from the pan and set aside.

Cook the pasta, following the packet instructions, until al dente.

Meanwhile, deglaze the frying pan with the prosecco, scraping up all the caramelised herbs and lobster from the bottom of the pan, then add the stock, bring to a strong simmer and reduce by half. Add the onion, chilli and zucchini and simmer for about 10 minutes, then add the remaining 3 tablespoons of butter, allow it to melt and gently simmer for a few minutes more. Add the beans and remaining tarragon and coriander, give it all a stir and taste for seasoning—add salt if needed but I don't use any pepper in this dish.

Add the lobster to the sauce to heat through. Drain the pasta and add to the pan. Toss well to coat the pasta, then add half the tomato and mix through.

Serve in big bowls and garnish with a little chopped tarragon, coriander and the remaining tomato dice.

Feeds 4

This is a dish I pinched off my wife who is the master at cooking it. She normally adds new season asparagus instead of zucchini, and I've added some wine to mine—since I first experimented with the dish at a winery. I'm very pleased with how my version turned out but, truth be told, I like nothing better than when my wife cooks her version for me!

SMOKED TROUT PASTA

375 g (13 oz) linguine or spaghetti
1 tablespoon butter
1 red onion, thinly sliced
2 garlic cloves, finely chopped
8 baby zucchini (courgettes) with flowers
125 ml (4 fl oz/½ cup) rosé wine

300 ml (10½ fl oz) pouring cream
1 teaspoon dijon mustard
200 g (7 oz) smoked trout, deboned and flaked
2 tablespoons wild fennel or fennel tips
salt and freshly ground black pepper
2 large tomatoes, peeled, seeded and finely diced

Fill a large saucepan with water and add a very generous pinch of salt. Bring to the boil over high heat and then add the pasta. Stir so that it doesn't stick and then while it cooks give it a stir every few minutes. Cook according to the packet instructions until *al dente*—if you put the pasta on and then cook the dish, the pasta should be ready at the right time to drain and add to the sauce.

Meanwhile, heat the butter in a saucepan over medium–high heat. When beginning to foam, add the onion and cook for several minutes or until it becomes translucent, then add the garlic and cook for a few minutes more.

Remove the flowers from the zucchini and reserve for garnish. Roughly chop the zucchini and add to the pan, then cook for 3–4 minutes until softened. Add the wine, bring to the boil and reduce by half. Reduce the heat to medium and add the cream and mustard, and simmer for several minutes. Add the trout and warm through. Add the wild fennel or fennel tips, season with salt and black pepper and stir.

Use tongs to add the pasta to the smoked trout sauce, give it all a good toss to combine, then add the tomato. Divide between four bowls and garnish with the torn zucchini flowers.

Serve with crusty bread and a chilled bottle of rosé.

Feeds 4

 198

This recipe to me is what is so great about true Italian cooking—keeping it simple, using only a few fantastic ingredients and letting the main ingredient do the talking. In this recipe the crab is the main ingredient but the squid ink pasta is its lover and together they make a wonderful marriage. You could go that extra step and make your own squid ink pasta, but that can get pretty messy. You could also substitute the crab for some beautiful prawns and scallops. To me, this is a dish best served by candlelight with a lovely glass of wine and of course the person you love most in your life.

SPANNER CRAB WITH SQUID INK ANGEL HAIR PASTA

1 tablespoon olive oil
1 garlic clove, finely chopped
1 long red chilli, finely chopped
125 ml (4 fl oz/½ cup) dry white wine
2 tablespoons finely chopped flat-leaf (Italian) parsley, plus extra to garnish

salt and freshly ground white pepper
200 g (7 oz) spanner crab meat or blue swimmer crab meat
250 g (9 oz) squid ink angel hair pasta
2 teaspoons salmon roe*

Heat the olive oil in a frying pan over medium heat. Add the garlic and chilli and gently fry for a few minutes. Add the white wine and parsley, bring to a simmer and cook for a few minutes so the flavours combine, then season with salt and pepper. Add the crab meat and simmer gently for 3–4 minutes until the crab is just cooked.

Cook the pasta in boiling salted water, following the packet instructions until *al dente*. Drain and then add the pasta to the frying pan with the crab, mix through thoroughly then serve. Garnish with a little more parsley and the salmon roe.

Divide between two bowls and enjoy.

Feeds 2

NOTE

You can easily double this up to serve four or you can make as above and serve it to four as an entrée. You can buy 500 g (1 lb 2 oz) bags of beautiful frozen crab meat from your fishmonger; use what you need and freeze the rest for next time.

TIP
You can buy salmon roe in jars from speciality delis.

I love mussels! I don't really understand why more people don't cook them. They are not difficult to prepare, they taste great, they are really cheap and nowadays you can buy 1 kilo vacuum-sealed bags of cleaned, fresh—as in still alive—mussels which makes them even easier to use!

MUSSELS IN COCONUT AND BEER

2 tablespoons olive oil
2 garlic cloves, chopped
1 small red chilli, finely chopped
1 kg (2 lb 4 oz) mussels, scrubbed and debearded
330 ml (11¼ fl oz/1⅓ cups) white ale (such as Hoegaarden Wit Beer)
1 tablespoon unsalted butter
1 long green chilli, thinly sliced
2.5 cm (1 in) piece ginger, peeled
1 lemongrass stem, white part only

1 Lebanese eggplant (aubergine), halved lengthways and sliced into 5 mm (¼in) pieces
75 g (2⅔ oz/½ cup) frozen peas
6 kaffir lime leaves, middle vein removed, thinly sliced
250 ml (9 fl oz/1 cup) coconut milk
60 ml (2 fl oz/¼ cup) coconut cream
1 teaspoon fish sauce
small handful coriander (cilantro) leaves

Heat 1 tablespoon of the olive oil in a large saucepan over medium heat. Add half the garlic and the red chilli and cook for 1–2 minutes, stirring. Add the mussels and one-third of the beer, increase the heat to high, then put the lid on and bring to the boil. Cook for about 3–4 minutes, shaking the saucepan vigorously. Check to see if all or most of the mussels have opened, remove from the heat and pour the mussels into a colander sitting over a large bowl to capture all the cooking liquor.

Put the pan back on the stove, add the butter and remaining oil and when the butter is foaming add the rest of the garlic and the green chilli and stir. Smash the peeled ginger, then add to the pan. Peel away the tough outer layers of the lemongrass then use a sharp knife and trim off the base. Cut the stalk into four pieces and then smash the stem to bruise and release the flavour. Add to the pan. Add the eggplant, peas and kaffir lime leaves. Give it a stir and cook for 5 minutes. Add half of the remaining beer, the coconut milk, coconut cream and fish sauce and bring to the boil. Remove the colander with the mussels from the bowl and set aside. Strain the cooking liquor from the mussels through a fine-mesh sieve to remove any dirt, grit or bits of shell and then add to the pan. Bring to the boil, then reduce the heat slightly and simmer for a couple of minutes. Add the mussels and stir through, then simmer for 2 minutes. Taste the sauce for seasoning and adjust as necessary. Simmer for a couple more minutes.

Divide the mussels and sauce equally into two large bowls and garnish with some freshly chopped coriander. Serve with some toasted crusty sourdough.

Feeds 2 as a main or 4 as an entrée

This is one-pot cooking and serving at its best and makes for a great dinner-party dish as everyone stands around the kitchen, beer or glass of wine in hand hungrily eyeing off the beautiful fresh crustaceans and talking while you get on with the cooking. This is a simple dish that relies, as always, on the freshness of its main ingredients—the crustaceans. To get the freshest you need to find, keep and treat very well a fishmonger who knows their stuff. Making your own curry powder from fresh ingredients will lift this recipe, however, you can find some great mixes online these days as well.

CRUSTACEAN CURRY

2 tablespoons peanut oil
1 red onion, diced
2 garlic cloves, chopped
2.5–3 cm (1–1¼ in) piece ginger, peeled and chopped
2 long green chillies, chopped
2 tablespoons curry powder
500 ml (17 fl oz/2 cups) coconut cream
500 ml (17 fl oz/2 cups) chicken stock

1 tablespoon tamarind pulp, soaked in 125 ml (4 fl oz/½ cup) hot water
3 zucchini (courgettes), cut into 1 cm (½ in) rounds
2 fresh spanner crabs, cleaned and cut*
12 large raw prawns (shrimp), peeled and deveined, tails intact
6 Balmain bug tails, tail meat removed and halved lengthways
25 g (1 oz/½ cup) chopped coriander (cilantro) leaves

Heat the peanut oil in a large saucepan over high heat. Add the onion and cook for several minutes, then add the garlic, ginger and chilli and cook, stirring, for a further 5 minutes. Add the curry powder and cook, stirring, until fragrant and well combined. Add the coconut milk and stock and stir well to get all of the spice mixed through. Bring to the boil, add the tamarind soaking liquid, but not the pulp, stir, then turn down the heat and simmer for 30 minutes or until the sauce has reduced by about one-third. Add the zucchini and cook for another 10 minutes or until the zucchini starts to soften. Add the crab, prawns and bug tails, stir through and cook for about 10 minutes. Add the chopped coriander and mix through.

I like to put the curry in the middle of the table for people to help themselves. Serve with white rice in bowls—I use an equal combination of basmati and jasmine rice cooked together as this adds a great texture.

Feeds 6–8

NOTE

Get your fishmonger to clean and prepare the crabs if you are unsure how to do it and, of course, mud crab or blue swimmer will be just as good as spanner crab.

I love to cook with beer, it's such a great ingredient in all sorts of dishes. Occasionally, I like to cook with some of the ingredients that go into making beer, such as hops. You can buy dried hop cones from your local home brew store or ask your friends if they home brew or know someone who does and then ask for a couple of hops! Get floral or aromatic hops as they will not be so bitter.

GOAN-STYLE FISH CURRY

60 ml (2 fl oz/¼ cup) olive oil
1 red onion, sliced
2 garlic cloves, thinly sliced
2 cm (¾ in) piece ginger, peeled and sliced
½ teaspoon ground turmeric
1 teaspoon cayenne pepper
400 ml (14 fl oz) coconut cream
200 ml (7 fl oz) stout
500 g (1 lb 2 oz) Jap pumpkin (winter squash),
    cut into small cubes
2 long green chillies, halved lengthways and
    chopped into quarters

1 lime
1 large tomato, cut into eighths
6 dried whole hop cones (optional)
300 g (10½ oz) tuna, cut into large pieces
250 g (9 oz) flathead fillets, cut into large pieces
250 g (9 oz) gurnard fillets, cut into large pieces
200 g (7 oz) squid, cut into large pieces and scored
75 g (2⅔ oz/½ cup) pepitas (pumpkin seeds), dry-
    roasted
15 g (½ oz/¼ cup) finely chopped coriander
    (cilantro) leaves

Heat the olive oil in a large flameproof casserole dish over high heat. Add the onion, reduce the heat to medium and cook, stirring occasionally, until the onion is caramelised. Add the garlic and ginger and cook for another 4–5 minutes, stirring. Add the spices and mix well to combine, then cook for several minutes until fragrant. Add the coconut cream, then add the stout, increase the heat and simmer, stirring well to mix the spices through the liquid. Add the pumpkin and bring back to a simmer. Put a lid on the dish and simmer gently for about 20–25 minutes, stirring occasionally. Remove the lid and allow the sauce to cook until all of the pumpkin has dissolved and thickened—what I will now call the gravy.

To finish the sauce, add the tomato, green chillies and a generous squeeze of lime juice. If you are using hop cones, put them in and leave to simmer for about 5 minutes. Keep tasting the sauce as the hops will add a lovely fruity flavour, but if left in too long they will also start to add quite a strong bitter character so it is best to remove them before that happens.

With the sauce on a gentle simmer, add the tuna and cook for a couple of minutes, then add the other fish and cook for 2–3 minutes before finally adding the squid. Turn up the heat to a more robust simmer, stir well and keep an eye on the fish so you don't overcook it. You can tell when the fish is ready if you press the fillets with your finger or a wooden spoon and they fall into flakes. There shouldn't be any rebound or firmness in the middle, if there is cook a little longer.

Serve over white rice and garnish with the roasted pepitas and some fresh chopped coriander.

Feeds 4–6

»»»»»»»»»»»»»»»»»»»»»
TIP
You can really use any fish you want to in this dish or you can make it with prawns, scallops, baby octopus or crab. The best advice I can give regarding what fish to use is go local and go fresh. I cook the tuna first as it is a heavier piece of fish where as the flathead and gurnard are both firm white-fleshed fish and will cook quicker than the tuna.
»»»»»»»»»»»»»»»»»»»»»

This cassoulet is my 'go to' winter dish as it's hearty, warming, filling, tasty and very versatile. Prosciutto-wrapped cod is a great addition, but equally I love cassoulet on its own or with spicy sausages cooked with the beans—adding another layer of flavour. Of course, you could make it a true cassoulet and confit some duck legs, then fry them off and serve them atop the beans—*fantastique*!

PROSCIUTTO-WRAPPED COD CASSOULET

80 ml (2½ fl oz/⅓ cup) olive oil

1 onion, chopped

100 g (3½ oz) pancetta, diced

2 garlic cloves, chopped into roughly 1 cm (½ in) pieces

1 carrot, chopped into roughly 1 cm (½ in) pieces

2 celery stalks, chopped into 1 cm (½ in) pieces

350 g (12 oz) cannellini beans, soaked overnight

500 mls (17 fl oz/2 cups) dry white wine, plus extra if needed

500 ml (17 fl oz/2 cups) chicken stock, plus extra if needed

3 rosemary sprigs

salt and freshly ground black pepper

4 cod fillets or another firm white-fleshed fish (about 150–180 g/5½–6¼ oz each)

4 long slices prosciutto

20 g (¾ oz/⅓ cup) chopped flat-leaf (Italian) parsley, plus extra to garnish

Heat 2 tablespoons of the olive oil in a saucepan over high heat. Add the onion and cook down until translucent. Add the pancetta and mix through for a few minutes, then add the garlic, carrot and celery. Sweat down for about 5 minutes, then drain the beans, add to the pan and mix through. Add enough wine and stock to cover the contents of the pan, bring to the boil then reduce the heat to a firm simmer. Add the rosemary and stir through. Stir the beans every 5–8 minutes, adding more stock and wine in equal amounts as needed to keep the mixture wet. Continue this process until the beans are cooked and tender—about 45 minutes or so. Add salt and black pepper to taste.

Meanwhile, season the cod with pepper and then wrap each fillet in a piece of prosciutto. It is best to do this not more than 5–10 minutes before cooking as the longer the fish stays wrapped in the prosciutto the more salty it will become.

Heat the remaining oil in a frying pan over medium–high heat. Lay the cod fillets in the pan, shake the pan to stop any sticking and cook for about 5 minutes until the prosciutto is browned and crisp. Gently turn the cod over and cook the other side for about 3–5 minutes or until golden brown and crisp and the cod is flaking.

Mix the chopped parsley through the cassoulet. Check the consistency—it should be moist but not wet, so cook out any excess liquid prior to serving.

Serve the cassoulet in the middle of each plate and then place a cod fillet on top. Garnish with a little extra parsley.

Feeds 4

I have a traditional paella pan that fits snugly on my kettle barbecue. When I cook my paella I drop pieces of hickory wood onto the hot coals which create lots of smoke, then I close the lid on the barbecue and let the smoke sink into the rice as it bubbles away—magnificent! If you can cook this paella over a fire the results are well worth the effort. In fact, the paella pan was designed to encourage barbecue smoke to come up the sides of the pan and into the dish.

SEAFOOD PAELLA WITH CHORIZO AND PEAS

2 litres (70 fl oz/8 cups) chicken stock

1.5 g (¹⁄₂₀ oz) saffron threads

3 small lobster tails (250–300 g/9–10½ oz each)

250 g (9 oz) squid tentacles or squid rings

80 ml (2½ fl oz/⅓ cup) olive oil

3 garlic cloves, finely chopped

2 red chillies, sliced

1 jar (110 g/3¾ oz) small capers in brine, drained

1 red capsicum (pepper), thinly sliced

2 chorizo sausages, cut diagonally into 5 mm (¼ in) thick pieces

1 tablespoon smoky paprika

1 small red chilli, thinly sliced (or as much or as little as you want)

1 tin (400 g/14 oz) chopped tomatoes

440 g (15½ oz/2 cups) Arroz Calasparra paella rice

500 g (1 lb 2 oz) pink snapper (or another firm white-fleshed fish), cut into bite-size pieces

10 raw prawns (shrimp)

250 g (9 oz) scallops

215 g (7⅔ oz/1½ cups) frozen peas

handful of caperberries

Put the stock in a saucepan and bring to a gentle simmer.

Soak the saffron in 60 ml (2 fl oz/¼ cup) of the stock for about 20 minutes.

Cut the lobster tails in half, lengthways, and then hold the tail ends and dip them in the hot stock for about 10–15 seconds—this makes it much easier to remove the meat from the tail shells. Remove the meat and roughly chop, then set aside. Put the empty shells in the stock to add extra flavour. If using squid rings, cut the rings in half so you have two long strips, then cut these strips in half lengthways into thinner strips. Set aside.

Place your paella pan over the hot coals or flames of your barbecue and heat 2 tablespoons of the olive oil in the pan. Add one-third of the chopped garlic, half the sliced red chilli and 2 tablespoons of the capers. When all are sizzling and mixed together add the chopped lobster. Cook, stirring well for several minutes until the lobster is almost cooked. Remove the lobster, chilli, garlic and capers, place in a bowl and set aside.

Heat the rest of the oil in the pan, then add the rest of the garlic and sliced chilli, another 2 tablespoons of the capers, the capsicum and the chorizo and fry for about 5 minutes, making sure to stir often so the garlic doesn't burn. Add the paprika and stir well so everything is well coated. Cook for a couple of minutes. Add the tomatoes and the saffron with its soaking liquid, mix well and bring to a simmer, then mix in the rice. Let the rice absorb any moisture from the tomatoes before adding 250 ml (9 fl oz/1 cup) of the simmering stock and mixing it through.

Traditionally, you are not supposed to stir a paella—just add all the stock and let it cook—but I tend to do mine a little more like a risotto, adding some stock, giving it a stir and letting it absorb into the rice, then adding another ladleful, giving it a stir … just like cooking any rice dish, you don't want it to cook too fast or too slow so keep an eye on it.

When you have used about three-quarters of your stock, add the snapper, mix through and cook for a couple of minutes, then add in another 250 ml of hot stock along with the prawns, scallops and squid—mix the seafood through so that it is covered by the rice and allow the stock to be absorbed. When the fish is almost cooked and the stock is absorbed, add another 250 ml of stock along with the peas and the reserved cooked lobster, chilli, garlic and capers, then mix through. By the time the stock is absorbed the fish should be cooked as should the rice. Taste and, if need be, add a little more stock until everything is cooked well. The paella should not be too moist or runny and the rice should still have a little bite to it. Scatter a handful or two of the caperberries over the paella and leave it on the heat for a couple of minutes to encourage a golden caramelised crust (called a socarrat) to form on the bottom of the pan—in Spain this is considered the best part.

Traditionally, you eat directly out of the pan with friends gathered around, so serve the dish by giving everyone a fork and encouraging them to dig in.

Feeds 8–10

Pancakes aren't just for breakfast—I reckon they are even better as a dessert, especially when they're made like this. The tannins in the tea complement the tartness in the raspberries and of course cream and fresh raspberries ... need I say more.

BLACK TEA PANCAKES WITH RASPBERRY CREAM

150 g (5½ oz/1 cup) self-raising flour
1 tablespoon caster (superfine) sugar
300 ml (10½ fl oz) milk
5 good quality black tea bags
2 tablespoons honey
1 free-range egg

3 tablespoons unsalted butter
300 ml (10½ fl oz) double cream (or clotted cream)
250 g (9 oz) raspberry coulis (or about 350 g/ 12 oz frozen berries, thawed, blended and pushed through a sieve)
1 punnet (125 g/4½ oz) raspberries

Put the flour and sugar in a large mixing bowl and mix to combine. Pour the milk into a glass measuring jug (pitcher) and then zap in the microwave for 1 minute so that it is quite warm but not really hot. Put the tea bags in and jiggle them for 1 minute then let them steep for another 5 minutes. Add the honey and stir to dissolve. Jiggle the bags some more, then squeeze them out so as to collect all the milk and flavour and then discard. Crack the egg into the cooled milky tea and beat. Use a whisk to slowly add the milk to the flour, and mix to form a batter.

Heat a non-stick frying pan over medium heat and add about ½ teaspoon of butter. When it has melted, swirl the pan to coat. Pour in some of the batter and cook until bubbles start to form on the top. Turn the pancake over with an egg slide and cook the other side. Remove the pancake to a plate and continue with the remaining mixture, putting a little bit of butter in the pan each time so the pancakes don't stick.

Put the cream in a bowl, add about 3 tablespoons of the coulis to the cream and gently swirl through. You can use more or less of the coulis depending on how much raspberry flavour you want to come through.

Stack one, two or three pancakes on each plate, spoon over some of the raspberry cream, scatter some fresh raspberries over and enjoy.

Makes about 12 pancakes

NOTE

If you only want to make a couple of pancakes you can reserve any leftover mixture covered in the fridge to use over the next couple of days.

This is a perfect summer dessert served up after a leisurely afternoon spent eating, drinking and enjoying the company of family and friends. It also has that wow factor which will bring giggles of delight and praise at the end of a dinner party. It is clean, fresh, fruity, has a hint of alcohol from the prosecco, spiciness from the sichuan pepper and bitterness from the ruby red grapefruit. Yes, it really is a slice of summer on a plate.

FRESH BERRY AND PROSECCO TERRINE

200 ml (7 fl oz) freshly squeezed ruby red
    grapefruit juice, strained
400 ml (14 fl oz) prosecco
2 tablespoons caster (superfine) sugar
½ teaspoon sichuan peppercorns, dry-fried
    and ground using a mortar and pestle

4 titanium-strength gelatine leaves
6 large mint leaves
4 very large strawberries, hulled and sliced
125 g (4½ oz) each of raspberries, blueberries and
    blackberries
3 nectarines, diced

Combine the grapefruit juice, prosecco, sugar and sichuan pepper in a saucepan and gently bring to the boil, stirring to dissolve the sugar. Taste to gauge the sweetness and, if need be, add a little more sugar. Remove from the heat and leave to cool a little.

Soak the gelatine in cold water for a few minutes until very soft, then squeeze out the excess water and add to the hot prosecco mixture. Stir gently to dissolve.

Line a 22 x 12 cm (8½ x 4½ in) terrine tin with plastic wrap so that it hangs well over the sides of the tin and place the mint leaves down the centre. Remember that the bottom of the tin will become the top or presentation side of the terrine when you turn it out. Next, place the strawberry slices over the mint leaves to cover the bottom of the tin. You can either place a complete layer of each fruit one after the other so that the terrine is nicely layered or you can mix the rest of the fruits together and just pile them into the tin—I prefer the mix method. Pour the prosecco and gelatine mixture carefully over the fruit to fill the tin. Fold over the overhanging plastic wrap and put in the fridge until set—generally overnight.

When you are ready to serve, turn out the terrine by dipping the tin very briefly in hot water and inverting it onto a plate or cutting board. Use a very sharp knife (also dipped first into hot water) to cut it into slices.

Serve with some ice cream, yoghurt or even a sabayon sauce and of course a glass of prosecco!

Feeds 8-10

CHAPTER 6

Feeding
THE RUG RATS

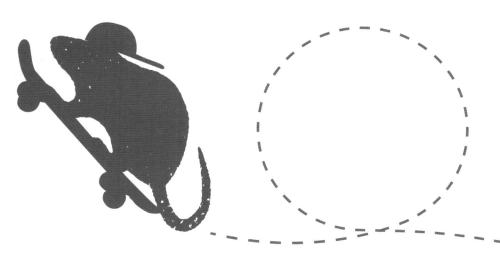

For me, feeding the rug rats is more about teaching them to cook rather than feeding them dinner. First and foremost, if you cook something they get excited about and really want to eat, they will also get excited about how it is made, which hopefully will lead to them wanting to cook it themselves. Well that's how it worked with my kids. Most of the recipes in this section have been typed up and put into each of my daughters' recipe books—by them—to be taken with them when they leave home, to be cooked by them, added to and changed according to their palates and will probably be passed on to their children just as my mum passed some of these recipes on to me.

As a parent there is no greater feeling than feeding your kids food that has been made with love and is full of goodness and nourishment that will help them to grow up to be healthy, happy and positive people. Well, actually, there is, and that is the joy of cooking with your kids! Yes, it can get very messy—which is usually left to you to clean up—and occasionally there are burnt fingers and scrapes, but that's just the way it is. Before you know it, your kids will be bringing you breakfast in bed or cooking you a three-course meal for dinner that tastes pretty damn good—perhaps even better than if you'd cook it—and that is just the way it should be.

Pancakes are really easy to make, can be served up with anything and are a good hearty breakfast, not to mention a great opportunity to get the kids in the kitchen and have a bit of shared cooking fun. Funnily enough, I have a friend who just can't cook pancakes and I think I know what his problem is—pan control! You need to get your pan up to the right temperature and then hold it there while you cook the ten or so pancakes that the mix will make. Usually, my first pancake is the 'tester' pancake and not the best one of the bunch, my last pancake is the 'great' pancake—not just because it is perfectly cooked, but because it's the last of the batter it is usually twice the size of the rest!

PANCAKES

150 g (5½ oz/1 cup) self-raising flour
2 tablespoons caster (superfine) sugar
1 free-range egg

300 ml (10½ fl oz) milk
unsalted butter, for frying

Put the flour in a large mixing bowl, add the sugar and mix together well.

Pour the milk into a large jug (pitcher), break the egg into the milk and use a fork to beat until combined. Use a whisk and gradually add the milk to the flour, whisking all the time, until well combined and smooth. You do not want a batter too thick as this will make thick dense pancakes, so add a little extra milk if need be. Nor do you want it too thin as you will get thin dry pancakes, so add a little more flour and whisk it in if required. Let the batter sit for 30 minutes if you can and you will find the batter will thicken up a little. You can use plain (all-purpose) flour, but the pancakes will not be as light and fluffy as ones made with self-raising flour.

Preheat the oven to 110°C (225°F) (fan-forced 90°C/195°F). Place a serving plate in the oven to warm.

So here is the scoop on cooking your pancakes to perfection—add a teaspoon of butter to a non-stick frying pan which should be sitting over medium heat. The butter shouldn't sizzle loudly and melt quickly as this means your pan is too hot. If you burn the butter you will need to wipe your pan clean and start again. The butter should melt in 20 or so seconds and you should swirl it around the pan �»➡

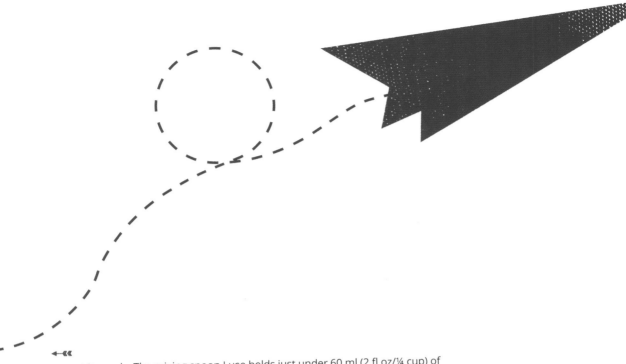

to coat it evenly. The mixing spoon I use holds just under 60 ml (2 fl oz/¼ cup) of liquid so let's just say tip almost 60 ml of pancake mix into the centre of the pan and then gently tip the pan in a circular motion so the pancake mixture spreads around and forms a circle about 15 cm (6 in) in diameter. Now just let it cook until you see little bubbles form all over the top of the pancake then, using a plastic egg slide or spatula, carefully work your way under the pancake—sometimes on the first pancake it will stick in the centre—get your egg slide all the way under and flip it over. The top should be nice and golden brown and feel soft. Cook for a minute or so and then take out of the pan and place on the plate in the oven to keep warm.

Now just repeat this process until there is no more pancake mix left, with the exception that I use a small knob of butter each time (not quite a teaspoon). So butter in, swirl around, pancake mix in, gentle circle motion, cook until bubbles appear, flip over, cook 1 minute, take out and put on top of the pancake already on the plate in the oven and close the oven door.

After you cook a few pancakes your frying pan will start to hold heat better and indeed get a little hotter, so you may need to turn the heat down a little to compensate. Also, if you find there is enough butter in the pan between some pancakes, then cook a pancake without adding butter first and it will use the excess in the pan before you add a knob of butter for the next one.

Serve the stack of pancakes in the middle of the table for people to help themselves. You could serve them with the blood orange curd (to the right) as I have done or see the note for other serving suggestions.

Feeds 4

NOTE

As for more toppings, my youngest daughter likes Vegemite on her pancakes, my other two daughters prefer a squeeze of lemon juice and a sprinkle of raw sugar. I love my pancakes with a strip or two of bacon and a drizzle of maple syrup over it all. Other toppings could include fresh berries, slices of banana, a drizzle of honey with some yoghurt, some ricotta cheese or cream cheese, or even smoked salmon with some goat's cheese and a drizzle of tzatziki! Almost anything goes, so go for it!

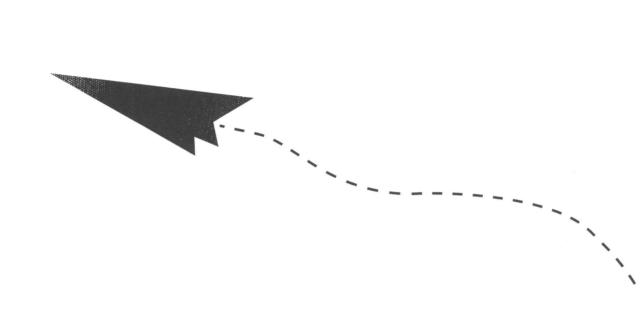

You can use this as a side for any of the fruit tarts in this book. You could have it on pancakes or you can go to your local gourmet deli and buy small pre-baked pastry cups and fill them with the curd. Then add some sliced fruit—think mango, pear, strawberries or white peaches—and serve with some ice cream. It is a good recipe to have in your arsenal, 'just in case', and it is easy to scale up if you want to make a big batch for a big tart or to fill a yellow layer cake.

BLOOD ORANGE CURD

125 ml (4 fl oz/½ cup) blood orange juice
110 g (3¾ oz/½ cup) caster (superfine) sugar
juice of ½ lime (about 2 teaspoons)

1 teaspoon grated blood orange zest
4 free-range egg yolks
70 g (2½ oz) unsalted butter, chopped

Put the blood orange juice, sugar, lime juice, zest and egg yolks in a saucepan and place over a gentle heat. Stir to combine and continue to mix as you need to keep it moving so the egg doesn't set on the bottom of the pan. Depending on the heat it may take 10–15 minutes for the curd to thicken, just keep stirring and watching until it gets to the thickness you require. Remove from the heat and gradually add the butter, stirring with a whisk to amalgamate the butter into the curd. Put the curd in a bowl, cover with plastic wrap (directly on the curd to stop a skin from forming) and set aside until you want to use it.

Makes about 250 g (9 oz/1 cup)

I call this the kitchen sink frittata because it has everything in it but the kitchen sink! The reason for that is because a frittata is the perfect dish to use up all those bits you have left over in your fridge after cooking various meals throughout the week. Of course, you don't have to make this exact frittata—you could make a simple asparagus and feta cheese frittata or go to town and make a big Tex-Mex frittata with beans, chorizo, tomato, onion, avocado, jalapeño and cheese! I have even heard of people using their leftover Thai takeaway as the main ingredients in a frittata—what a great idea! I cook this in a 22 cm (8½ in) frying pan with high-ish sides so I can get a nice deep frittata. I have also heard of people baking their frittata in a lined springform cake tin—I haven't tried this, but it sounds like a good idea, too.

THE KITCHEN SINK FRITTATA

60 ml (2 fl oz/¼ cup) olive oil

2 potatoes, peeled and diced into 5 mm (¼ in) cubes

1 garlic clove, crushed

1 chilli, finely chopped (or a sprinkle of chilli powder) (optional)

1 onion, sliced (or a couple of spring onions/ scallions, chopped)

2 capsicum (pepper) cheeks

1 chorizo, diced (or about 120 g/4¼ oz smoked chicken or salami)

about 160 g (5¾ oz/2 cups) mixed vegetables (such as beans, peas, carrot, zucchini/courgettes), all cut to the same size dice as the potato

6 free-range eggs

salt and freshly ground black pepper

10 g (¼ oz/¾ cup tightly packed) rocket (arugula) leaves

75 g (2⅔ oz/¾ cup) grated cheddar cheese

Preheat your grill (broiler) to high.

Heat 2 tablespoons of the olive oil in a 22 cm (8½ in) ovenproof frying pan over medium–high heat. Add the potato and fry, stirring, for about 8 minutes or until golden and crisp but still soft in the centre. Add the garlic and chilli and cook for a minute or so, mixing through the potato, then remove with a slotted spoon and drain on paper towel. If need be, add the remaining tablespoon of olive oil and when hot add the onion, capsicum and chorizo and cook for about 4–5 minutes or until the onion is starting to colour and the chorizo is crisp, then stir through the mixed vegetables and cook until the vegetables are softened.

While the vegetables cook, crack the eggs into a bowl, beat together and season with some salt and black pepper and any other spice or herb you want to use. I often spice my eggs with ground cumin, or you can mix through some finely chopped parsley, chives or coriander (cilantro) leaves. ➜➜

As a parent there is no greater feeling than feeding your kids ... Well, actually, there is, and that is the joy of cooking with your kids!

When the vegetables are done, return the potato and garlic back to the pan and mix through. Add the rocket, then pour the eggs into the pan and use a soft spatula to make sure the vegetables are evenly distributed. Sprinkle the cheese over the top. Use the spatula to gently move the eggs away from the sides of the pan and allow any runny egg mix to seep down and cook. As the frittata cooks and sets keep using the spatula to pull the frittata away from the side—this helps when it comes time to turn the frittata out of the pan. When the frittata is set, but still a bit wobbly, put the pan under the hot grill. Cook for about 5 minutes or until firmly set and nicely brown on the top. Return to the stove over medium heat and carefully use a spatula to push around and under the frittata to make sure it is not stuck to the bottom of the pan.

Now comes the fun part. You could slide the frittata out onto a plate although sometimes they will split or fall apart, which is quite annoying. Instead, put a serving plate, top side down, on top of the frittata and, holding the plate firmly, flip it and the frying pan over. Hopefully, the frittata will fall out off the pan and is now sitting nicely on the plate! The only thing now is you have the bottom of the frittata facing the wrong way up, so take another serving plate and place it upside down on the frittata and repeat the turning process so you will now have the frittata up the right way with the lovely browned top facing up.

Eat!

I like to serve this with some hot mango chutney on the side.

Feeds 6

This is my 'go to' salad when the family are having anything on the barbecue—chicken, quail, prawns (shrimp), snags, steak, burgers, lamb backstrap ... you name it. It's a simple salad that has a lovely depth of flavours—acid from the tomatoes, earthiness from the beetroot, sweetness from the corn, spiciness from the onion ... It's my 'go to' salad because I love it and so will you.

SPRING SALAD

150 g (5½ oz) mixed salad lettuce
1 small red onion, thinly sliced
1 tin (420 g/4¼ oz) unsalted corn kernels, drained
1 punnet (200 g/7 oz) cherry tomatoes, halved
1 tin (420 g/4¼ oz) baby beetroot (beets), drained
   then halved or quartered depending on size
1 large carrot, grated or julienned if you have a
   julienne peeler
1 red capsicum (pepper), thinly sliced
2 Lebanese (short) cucumbers, peeled, halved
   lengthways and thinly sliced

Dressing
2 tablespoons olive oil
1 tablespoon balsamic vinegar
1 tablespoon red wine vinegar
1 garlic clove, crushed
1 teaspoon wholegrain mustard
1 teaspoon honey
salt and freshly ground black pepper

Give your lettuce a good wash to make sure there isn't any dirt in it, then give it a good dry in your lettuce spinner or between sheets of paper towel. If your lettuce is wet the dressing won't stick to it—oil and water don't mix! Throw everything into a large salad bowl and give it a mix.

To make the dressing, put all the ingredients in a clean jar, including a pinch of salt and several turns of freshly ground black pepper. Put the lid on and then give the jar a really good shake to completely combine. Remove the lid and stick your finger into the dressing to taste. It should be well balanced between the oil and the vinegar, the garlic should be mild and tempered by the mustard and the dressing slightly sweet from the honey. Pour over the salad and mix well.

Feeds 4

When I was shooting my TV show, occasionally I would go to a farm with a dish in mind to prepare only to find they didn't have some or all of the ingredients I wanted for the dish. This salad is a case in point. The ingredients in this salad were all the ingredients that were growing in the veggie patch. In fact, they also grew chickens, so I was also able to make a version with chicken in it too!

TASSIE GARDEN SALAD

2 fresh corn on the cob
2 tablespoons butter
90 g (3 oz/2 cups) baby English spinach leaves
4 tomatoes, cut into eighths
½ red onion, thinly sliced
3 spring onion (scallions), thinly sliced
1 large carrot, grated
1 large yellow zucchini (cougette), grated
1 telegraph (long) cucumber, finely diced
1 beetroot (beet), peeled and grated

Dressing
2 garlic cloves
½ teaspoon salt
60 ml (2 fl oz/¼ cup) olive oil
60 ml (2 fl oz/¼ cup) balsamic vinegar
freshly ground black pepper

Preheat the barbecue hotplate to high.

Butter the corn, season with salt and then char on the barbecue until cooked on all sides. Cut the corn off the cob and set aside.

Put all the other ingredients in a salad bowl and give it a good mix to evenly combine.

To make the dressing, cream the garlic with the salt using the back of a large kitchen knife or using a mortar and pestle. Combine with the olive oil and balsamic, season, then pour over the salad.

Feeds 4

NOTE

To turn this into a chicken salad, marinate four free-range chicken marylands on the bone in my herb–marinated barbecued chicken marinade on page 142 and then barbecue until perfectly cooked. Slice the meat off the bone and mix through the salad.

On a hot summer's night when you don't want to cook inside and just want something light, tasty, no mess and no fuss I say cook this! It is a great salad and is super easy to scale up if you have a whole lot of people coming over to have a swim in your pool! If you don't have a pool it's a great salad to take with you when you drop in your friends who do have one. How could they say no!

BARBECUED SEAFOOD SALAD

80 ml (2½ fl oz/⅓ cup) olive oil, plus extra for grilling
2 tablespoons lemon juice
1 garlic clove, crushed
1 tablespoon Thai-style sweet chilli sauce
1 tablespoon chopped basil
¼ teaspoon dried chilli flakes
salt and freshly ground black pepper
12 raw prawns (shrimp), peeled and deveined, tails left intact
12 scallops (with or without roe)
1 squid tubes

2 red emperor fillets (about 180–200 g/6¼–7 oz each) (or snapper, perch or blue-eye)
½ red onion, sliced
1 baby fennel bulb, sliced
1 baby cos (romainne) lettuce, washed and leaves torn
1 radicchio, washed and leaves torn
1 punnet (200 g/7 oz) cherry tomatoes, halved
2 pieces marinated roasted red capsicum (pepper), sliced
2 tablespoons sherry vinegar

Put 2 tablespoons of the olive oil, the lemon juice, garlic, sweet chilli sauce, basil and chilli flakes in a large bowl. Season with salt and pepper and mix well, then add the prawns and scallops and mix so the seafood is well coated.

Lay the squid tube flat on your work surface and cut into two equal-sized pieces. Rinse the squid under cold water and remove any cartilage. Score the inside of the hoods in a diagonal pattern without cutting all the way through—this will allow the squid to curl during cooking. Cut each piece into strips about 1 cm (½ in) wide and 3 cm (½ –1¼ in) long and add to the marinade. Cut the fish fillets into bite-sized pieces and add to the marinade. Mix well, cover with plastic wrap and place in the fridge to marinate for a couple of hours.

Preheat the barbecue hotplate to high, season with olive oil, then add the red onion and fennel and fry until softened and coloured. Remove from the heat and put in a salad bowl with the cos, radicchio, cherry tomatoes and capsicum, and mix well. Use tongs to pick the fish out of the marinade and put on the hotplate, followed by the prawns, squid and then the scallops. Cook, turning often and basting with some of the marinade, until the seafood is perfectly cooked—the fish should flake if you push it with your tongs, the prawns and scallops should have some nice colour but still remain soft, and the squid should only need 1–2 minutes. Remove from the heat and set aside to cool down for a couple of minutes before adding to the bowl with the salad and giving it a good toss.

For the dressing, put the remaining olive oil and the sherry vinegar in a jar. Season with salt and pepper and give it a good shake to combine. Pour over the salad and serve.

Feeds 4

This is a family favourite and one that my daughters have handwritten into their own personal cookbooks to be taken with them on their travels through life. I know they'll be cooking it for their kids, which is a pretty satisfying feeling. The use of parsnip and turnip adds a lovely earthiness to this soup. I always use chicken stock, but you can use vegetable if you want a veggie option.

MINESTRONE SOUP

1 tablespoon olive oil
1 tablespoon butter
3 celery stalks, diced
1 large leek, white part only, sliced
2 carrots, diced
1 turnip, peeled and diced
1 medium or 2 small parsnips, diced
2 large potatoes, peeled and diced

2 litres (70 fl oz/8 cups) chicken stock
  (preferably homemade)
1 tin (440 g/15½ oz) chopped tomatoes
1 bouquet garni
3 bay leaves
salt and freshly ground black pepper
5 silverbeet (Swiss chard) leaves, washed, white
  stem removed, thinly sliced

Heat the olive oil and butter in a large flameproof casserole dish over medium–high heat. Add the leek, stir to coat well and then reduce the heat to medium and cook, stirring often, until the leek becomes translucent. The longer you cook it the more sweetness you get from it, which is good. Add the carrot and celery, mix thoroughly, and cook for 5–8 minutes. Add the turnip, parsnip and potato, mix thoroughly, increase the heat to medium–high and cook for about 5 minutes, stirring often. Add the stock and stir through the veggies, then bring to the boil. Add the tomatoes, bouquet garni and bay leaves. Taste and add salt and pepper as required. Give it all a mix, turn the heat down to a simmer and cook for 20–30 minutes, then add the silverbeet, mix through well and cook for about 5 minutes until the veggies are tender. Serve with crusty bread.

Feeds 6

NOTE

Instead of silverbeet you can add 45 g (1½ oz/1 cup of chopped spinach and 50 g (1¾ oz/½ cup) of frozen peas. You can beef this soup up if you want by adding 175 g (6 oz/1 cup) of cooked shredded chicken or even some chicken mince that has been cooked off in a little garlic and olive oil. For the stock, homemade is always best, however, for busy people there are some great stocks on the market in both liquid and powder form, some, even though they are a chicken stock, are actually meat free and gluten free.

This is another terrific hand-me-down family recipe that my mum made for me, I make for my kids and they will no doubt make for theirs. Funnily enough, my wife saw me writing this and said that this is her mum's recipe that her mum made for her and then my wife made for our kids! It doesn't really matter whose recipe it is, as it's now yours! If you have any meat sauce left over it is great on toast for lunch the next day. Our favourite pasta shape for this was the shell-shape one and, on occasion, just to change it up, we would go with spirals.

MY MUM'S BOLOGNESE

1 tablespoon olive oil

1 brown onion, diced

2 garlic cloves, finely chopped

1 teaspoon dried basil

20 kalamata olives (I leave them whole, but you
    can pit and halve them if you like)

3 tablespoons tomato paste (concentrated purée)

650 g (1 lb 7 oz) minced (ground) beef

60 ml (2 fl oz/¼ cup) dry red wine

2 tins (800 g /1 lb 15 oz) crushed tomatoes

salt and freshly ground black pepper

pinch of sugar

2–3 bay leaves

freshly grated parmesan cheese

500 g (1 lb 2 oz) pasta shape of your choice

Heat the olive oil in a flameproof casserole dish over medium–high heat. Add the onion and cook gently for 5 minutes, stirring. Add the garlic and the dried basil and cook for another couple of minutes, then add the olives and heat through (my wife likes to add the olives when she adds the tomatoes). Add the tomato paste and cook for 2–3 minutes, stirring to combine, then add the mince. Turn the heat to high and use the back of a wooden spoon to break up the mince up so it doesn't clump, and then stir to evenly cook. Once all the meat is browned, turn the heat down to medium–high, add the wine and mix through, then add the tomatoes and 125 ml (4 fl oz/½ cup) of water. Bring the mixture to the boil, then reduce the heat to a simmer, season with salt, black pepper and sugar and add the bay leaves, then cook for 30 minutes or so, stirring occasionally.

Cook the pasta in plenty of boiling salted water, following the packet instructions. When the pasta is *al dente* drain in a colander then return to the saucepan you boiled it in. Add two or three spoonfuls of the sauce to the pasta and mix well—my wife doesn't like to do this but I do it so the noodles don't stick together after you've drained them. Divide the pasta between four bowls, ladle over a generous amount of the sauce, sprinkle with the parmesan and enjoy with a nice glass of red! Well, you, but not the kids.

Feeds 4

NOTE

You can make this with beef, pork or veal mince or even a combination of one or all of those. Being that I am a chilli head I would also add a small chopped red chilli to this recipe or a pinch of dried crushed chillies. You can also fill this out and satisfy any urges for vegetables by adding 1 cup each of grated carrot and grated zucchini (courgette) after you have cooked the onion for 5 minutes.

The thing with risotto is that everyone has their own way of doing it. Some people prefer their risotto quite dry, others quite wet, some don't like wine, other prefer vegetable stock to chicken stock ... The main thing to cooking a good risotto is experience, and through that finding your own preferences. Once you have mastered the basics a whole new world of food flavours will open up.

CHICKEN RISOTTO WITH SPINACH AND PEAS

2 litres (70 fl oz/8 cups) chicken stock
2 tablespoons olive oil
12 chicken tenderloins (about 600 g/1 lb 5 oz)
1 teaspoon garlic powder
½ teaspoon ground cumin
salt and freshly ground black pepper
1 tablespoon butter

1 small brown onion, diced
300 g (10½ oz) arborio rice
250 ml (9 fl oz/1 cup) white wine
60 g (2¼ oz/1½ cups) roughly chopped English spinach
140 g (5 oz/1 cup) frozen peas, thawed
3–4 tablespoons freshly grated parmesan cheese

Put the stock in a pot and simmer over low heat.

Heat 1 tablespoon of the olive oil in a large saucepan over medium–high heat. Add the chicken and fry, stirring for a minute, then add the garlic powder, cumin and seasoning. Continue to cook for 2 minutes, stirring to combine the flavours. When the chicken is almost cooked remove the pan from the heat, put the chicken in a bowl and keep warm.

Return the pan to the heat, add the butter and remaining oil and when hot add the onion and gently fry for about 3 minutes. Add the rice and mix so the rice is well coated and toasty hot, then add the wine. Mix well and let the wine absorb into the rice. When most of the wine has been absorbed add a ladleful of stock and reduce the heat to medium. For the next 25 minutes or so continue to stir the rice, adding a ladleful of stock each time the stock added prior is absorbed. If the stock is being absorbed too fast, turn the heat down, if it's absorbed too slowly turn the heat up—I guess this is where experience comes in, and you are on your way to getting experience! Let's say you should add a ladleful of stock every 5 or so minutes. After you have added the sixth ladleful of stock add the spinach and the peas, and stir well to combine. After you add in the seventh, stir through the cooked chicken and allow the stock to be absorbed. Taste the rice and see if it is cooked through—it shouldn't be soft and mushy, rather it should still have a little bit of firmness or bite to it. Add in the eighth ladleful of stock, stir through and allow it to be absorbed by the rice. You should have a nice thick porridge kind of consistency—which is what I like and is the traditional result. When you are happy with the consistency, remove from the heat, stir through the parmesan and serve.

Feeds 4

I love a good stir-fry and cook them often. The one problem I have with them is deciding what stir-fry to make! Prawn (shrimp) and squid with zucchini and beans, sichuan pork with shiitake mushrooms, bok choy and ginger, beef and broccoli … see what I mean?

SOY CHICKEN AND GARLIC STIR-FRY

175 ml (5½ fl oz) soy sauce

1 teaspoon garlic powder

2 skinless chicken breasts (about 300 g/ 10½ oz each), thinly sliced

2 tablespoons olive oil or peanut oil

1 red onion, halved lengthways then cut each half in half again to make four pieces

2 cheeks yellow capsicum (pepper), thinly sliced

1 carrot, finely chopped into thin matchsticks

1 garlic clove, crushed

1.5 cm (⅝ in) piece of ginger, peeled and thinly sliced

1–2 small red chillies, finely chopped (optional)

1 bunch broccolini, chopped

16 snow peas (mangetout), top and tailed

16 sugarsnap peas, top and tailed

2 bunches of baby bok choy (pak choy), stems cut off, leaves washed

2 tablespoons oyster sauce

1 tin (400 g/14 oz) stir-fry mixed vegetables*

Combine 125 ml (4 fl oz/½ cup) of the soy sauce and the garlic powder in a bowl. Add the sliced chicken and stir to coat well. Set aside and let it marinate while you prepare all the other ingredients.

Heat 1 tablespoon of the olive oil in a wok over high heat. When very hot add the chicken, being careful not to tip in all the soy sauce. Discard the remaining soy sauce marinade. Use a metal wok stirrer, tongs or a large metal spoon and move the chicken around so that it all sizzles madly and doesn't stick to the wok. Cook for a couple of minutes to sear, then put the chicken in the bowl you marinated it in, minus the soy sauce. You don't need to cook the chicken all the way through, as you will be adding it to the stir-fry at the end to finish it off.

Put the wok back on the heat, heat the remaining oil then add the onion. Move it around to coat in the oil and get it cooking. After a couple of minutes add the capsicum, carrot, garlic, ginger and chilli, if using, and cook, moving them around so they do not stick or burn. Turn the heat down a little and cook for a couple of minutes. Stir in the broccolini, snow peas, sugarsnap peas and bok choy. Add the remaining soy sauce, the oyster sauce and a tablespoon of water. Mix well, reduce the heat to medium and put the lid on so the veggies can steam a little. Cook for several minutes, then add the mixed stir-fry veggies and mix through. When the bok choy has wilted and the vegetables are tender but still have a slight crunch to them, return the chicken to the wok, turn the heat to high, and heat through. When the chicken is hot the stir-fry is done. Divide between four bowls.

I like this as is but you can serve it on rice or you can add rice noodles into the stir-fry.

Feeds 4

NOTE

You can buy tinned stir-fry mixed vegetables from the Asian section at your supermarket. They contain bamboo shoots, bean sprouts, corn and water chestnuts, and come in convenient amounts, just perfect for this recipe.

I kind of feel like I'm cheating with this soup as I'm not making my own wontons, but then that is the point of this soup—it is super easy. That said, if you really want to make your own wontons with the help of the rug rats, it's a fun project for a weekend afternoon! This is a great soup to make in bulk and then freeze in 1 litre (35 fl oz/4 cup) batches for use whenever you feel like it.

SUPER EASY WONTON SOUP

2 litres (70 fl oz/8 cups) chicken stock

2 tablespoons olive oil (or peanut oil)

1 large leek, white part only, halved lengthways and sliced

100 g (3½ oz) vermicelli rice noodles

2 tablespoons freshly sliced ginger

2 garlic cloves, finely chopped

60–80 ml (2–2½ fl oz/¼–⅓ cup) soy sauce

2 teaspoons fish sauce

2 bunches bok choy (pak choy) (it usually comes in three pieces per bunch)

16–20 frozen pork or prawn (shrimp) wontons

2 red bird's-eye chillies, cut in half lengthways (optional)

4 spring onions (scallions), sliced on the diagonal, to garnish

Put the stock in a large pot and bring to the boil over high heat, then reduce the heat so the stock is just simmering.

Heat the olive oil in a large saucepan or pot—it needs to be big enough to hold all the stock—over medium heat. When hot, add the leek and gently fry for 5 or so minutes, stirring occasionally.

Meanwhile, put the dried noodles in a bowl, cover with boiling water and set aside, stirring every now and then so they separate.

Add the ginger and garlic to the leek and fry for another 5 minutes or so, stirring occasionally, then add the hot stock and bring to a very gentle simmer. Add the soy sauce and fish sauce and taste—the soy will add a salty character, so you want to be able to taste it, and it should be in balance with the fish sauce. Add a little at a time as you can always add more, but you can't take it out! Let the soup simmer gently for 20–30 minutes to develop flavour.

Trim the white stalks off the bok choy, wash the leaves well, then cut into thirds. You can thinly slice some of the white stalk ends to put in the soup—just make sure you give them a good rinse as well. Add the bok choy leaves and the sliced stems to the pan and cook for a couple of minutes. Add the wontons and bring the heat up a little so that it comes to a more robust simmer, and simmer until the wontons are hot—about 5–8 minutes.

Drain the noodles and divide between four large bowls—you can use some of the noodle soaking water to add to the soup if you need a little more liquid, discard the rest. If using chillies, I like to add them into the bowls with the noodles, that way when you pour the hot stock over them they release their flavour and heat into the soup. Divide the wontons and bok choy equally between the bowls, ladle in the hot soup, garnish with the chopped spring onions and eat.

Feeds 4

NOTE

Dried vermicelli rice noodles are very thin rice noodles

My mum has made me this dish ever since I can remember and I have made it for my children ever since they can remember, and still do. It is one of those dishes that will be handed down to their children so when they come home from school and ask what's for dinner they'll sometimes be greeted with 'chicken with red rice' and the smile on their faces will say it all.

CHICKEN WITH RED RICE AND CORN

1 tablespoon olive oil
1 brown onion, diced
1 garlic clove, crushed
2 tablespoons tomato paste (concentrated purée)
1 tin (400 g/14 oz) chopped tomatoes
60 ml (2 fl oz/¼ cup) dry red wine (optional)
3 dried bay leaves

2 free-range chicken breasts (if you have it on the bone you will get more flavour)
salt and freshly ground black pepper
200 g (7 oz/1 cup) basmati or jasmine rice
170 g (6 oz/1 cup) Spanish stuffed green olives
1 tin (400 g/14 oz) corn kernels, drained
32 green beans, top and tailed, cut into thirds

Heat the olive oil in a flameproof casserole dish over medium heat. Add the onion and gently fry for 5 minutes or so, stirring. Once the onion is translucent, add the garlic and cook, stirring, for another 5 minutes, then add the tomato paste and stir well, cooking for several minutes. Next, add the tomatoes, wine and bay leaves and stir to combine. Bring to a simmer then add 500 ml (17 fl oz/2 cups) of boiling water and the chicken, and season with salt and pepper. Bring back to a simmer, reduce the heat so that the liquid simmers very gently, put the lid on and let the chicken cook for about 8 minutes then turn it over and cook for a further 8 minutes. When the chicken is still a little undercooked—we are going to return it to the dish later—remove it from the sauce and keep warm, covered, on a plate.

Add the rice to the dish, stirring it through, then increase the heat to a gentle but constant simmer and cook for 15 minutes, stirring occasionally to stop the rice from sticking to the bottom of the dish. Add the olives, corn and beans and stir through, then continue to cook until the rice is just cooked. You will need to add some more boiling water to the rice as you cook it—say 125 ml (4 fl oz/½ cup). Shred the chicken, discarding the bones and any skin and then return it to the dish along with any juice on the plate the chicken rested on and stir through. The rice mixture should be wet, but not sloppy. Once the chicken has heated through it is ready to serve.

Divide equally between four or six plates.

Feeds 4–6

»»»»»»»»»»»»»»»»»»»»
TIP
I always seem to make too much of this dish, which is great as I love to eat the leftovers the next day in a jaffle—it does make the best jaffle!
»»»»»»»»»»»»»»»»»»»»

I originally created this dish for my cooking show when we were filming in Cairns in Queensland. The episode featured various unique ingredients that I had never cooked with before, including crocodile. So yes, I cooked this dish with crocodile and you can too if you want to, although it may be a little hard to get. That said, I think it is better suited to pork neck or chicken thighs! Oh, and if you want to know what crocodile tastes like, it is a little like chicken with a texture a bit like firm white fish—weird.

PORK AND MANGO CURRY

2 tablespoons olive oil

1 red onion, sliced

½ red capsicum (pepper), cut into thin strips

50 g (1¾ oz) red curry paste (store-bought is fine)

700 g (1 lb 9 oz) pork neck, diced into 4–5 cm (1½–2 in) cubes (I like my curry meat to be cut into big chunks)

30 g (1 oz) piece of tamarind pulp, soaked and strained to yield about 80 ml (2½ fl oz/⅓ cup) of tamarind liquor

1 large mango, peeled and flesh squeezed into a bowl and then mashed to a pulp (or you can use 3 frozen mango cheeks)

300 ml (10½ fl oz) coconut milk

4 kaffir lime leaves, middle vein removed

1 lemongrass stem, white part only, finely chopped

16 snow peas (mangetout), top and tailed

16 green beans, top and tailed

½ zucchini (courgette), cut into sticks

1 Lebanese eggplant (aubergine), ends trimmed, halved lengthways and chopped

10 g (¼ oz/⅓ cup) coriander (cilantro) leaves, chopped

370 g (13 oz/2 cups) cooked rice, to serve (I always use a half-and-half mix of jasmine and basmati)

Preheat the oven to 180°C (350°F) (fan-forced 160°C/315°F).

Heat the olive oil in a large flameproof casserole dish over medium–high heat. Add the onion and capsicum and cook until the onion starts to turn golden. Add the curry paste and cook for several minutes, stirring, then add the pork and mix to coat the meat well. Cook for about 5 minutes, stirring all the time. Add the tamarind liquor, stir through, and cook for 3–4 minutes, stirring constantly. Add the mango pulp and coconut milk, stir to combine, then add the kaffir lime leaves and lemongrass, stir and bring to the boil. Put the lid on, transfer to the oven and cook for 1½ hours.

Remove the dish from the oven, add the vegetables, giving it a good stir, then return to the oven, covered, and cook for another 30 minutes or until the pork is cooked through—it should be very tender and the vegetables should also be cooked through.

Remove from the oven and stir through most of the chopped coriander. Divide the rice between four bowls, spoon over the curry, and serve with some more coriander.

Feeds 4

Lots of lovely simple flavours make these fish cakes very moreish. Strangely, I always think of fish patties as kids' food but I have to say when I make these I love them and always make sure I hide at least one away for a quiet snack the next day—yes they are delicious cold!

FISH AND VEGGIE PATTIES

2 potatoes (about 250 g/9 oz), peeled and chopped
1 parsnip (about 120 g/4¼ oz), chopped
200 g (7 oz) Jap (Kent) pumpkin (winter squash), peeled and chopped
salt
1 tablespoon butter
1 tablespoon olive oil, plus extra to shallow fry
225 g (8 oz) ocean trout or Atlantic salmon fillets
225 g (8 oz) firm white-fleshed fish fillets (such as barramundi, perch, rock ling or snapper)

½ teaspoon garlic powder
1 tablespoon chopped dill
freshly ground black pepper
3 spring onions (scallions), chopped
7 g (¼ oz/¼ cup) coriander (cilantro) leaves
1 free-range egg
zest of 1 large lemon or 2 small ones (about 1 heaped tablespoon)
70 g (2½ oz/½ cup) grated zucchini (courgette)
120 g (4¼ oz/2 cups) fresh breadcrumbs

Put the potato, parsnip and pumpkin in a saucepan, cover with cold water, add a generous pinch of salt and bring to the boil over high heat. Cook until tender, drain and mash, then set aside to cool.

If the fish has skin on then remove the skin and discard. Heat the butter and olive oil in a frying pan over medium–high heat, then add the fish fillets and cook for several minutes. Season the top of the fish with half the garlic powder, half the dill and some black pepper. Turn the fish over and season the cooked side with the rest of the garlic powder, dill and some more black pepper. Add one-third of the chopped spring onions to the pan. When the fish is cooked and easily flakes put it in a bowl and flake with a fork. Add the cooked spring onions and leave to cool.

Put the mashed veg, remaining spring onions, coriander, zest, zucchini and egg in a large mixing bowl and mix well. Add the flaked fish and gently mix through. Add 30 g (1 oz/½ cup) of the breadcrumbs and mix through. Season as needed.

Pour the rest of the breadcrumbs onto a plate. Wet your hands and take a handful of the fish and potato mixture and gently form a patty about 9–10 cm (3½–4 in) wide and about 3 cm (1¼ in) thick. Put the patty on the breadcrumbs, press gently to completely cover, gently shake off the excess then put the patty on a clean plate. Repeat with the rest of the mixture—you should have eight patties.

Heat enough olive oil in a large frying pan over medium–high heat to shallow-fry the patties—say about 1.5 cm (⅝ in) deep. When the oil is hot and it begins to shimmer, carefully add four of the patties and fry until golden brown and crunchy on both sides—turn the patties three times so each side gets two goes in the oil. Place the cooked patties on paper towel to drain, covered, while you cook the remaining patties. Serve with a salad.

Feeds 4

NOTE

Parsnip takes longer to cook than potato, and pumpkin cooks faster than potato, so cut your parsnip into smaller cubes and your pumpkin into larger cubes than the potato and it should all be done at the same time.

Tuesday night in our house when I was a kid was hamburger night, which was always exciting and something we all got up and pitched in to help with. Inevitably, whoever was toasting the buns would burn them, and would then have to scrape the burnt bits off with a butter knife to salvage them. It was always a happy time, burger nights.

MY MUM'S BEEF BURGERS

650 g (1 lb 7 oz) lean minced (ground) beef
1 brown onion, finely diced
2 garlic cloves, very finely diced
3 tablespoons tomato sauce
2 tablespoons worcestershire sauce
1 free-range egg
½ teaspoon mixed dried herbs
salt and freshly ground black pepper
80 ml (2½ fl oz/⅓ cup) olive oil
sliced cheddar cheese
hamburger buns

Toppings (optional)
tomato sauce (or chilli sauce or my smoky
     barbecue sauce on page 82)
fried bacon rashers
2–3 slices tomato
fried eggs
tinned beetroot slices
grated carrot
cucumber slices
lettuce

Put the beef mince, onion, garlic, sauces, egg, dried herbs, a pinch of salt and pepper in a large mixing bowl and use your hands to mix everything together. Cover with plastic wrap and leave to stand for 30–60 minutes.

Put the olive oil in a non-stick frying pan over medium–high heat. While waiting for the oil to come up to temperature take a handful of the mince mixture and form into a large ball and then flatten it down to make a patty about 2 cm (¾ in) thick—it should be a little larger than your hand. The patties shrink as they cook so don't be worried if the patties are larger than the hamburger buns at this stage. Carefully place your patty into the hot oil and repeat the process. I can normally fit three patties at a time into my frying pan. Cook for several minutes, then flip over and cook for another 3–4 minutes, turn the heat down to medium and cook gently turning two more times until the patties are cooked through.

On the last turning put slices of cheddar cheese on top of the burger (usually 3–4 slices will cover the top) and let that melt before removing the patties from the pan. Put the cooked patties on a plate and repeat with the rest of the mixture— you should have six to eight patties depending on how big you shape them.

To make the burgers, cut your hamburger buns in half and lightly toast both sides—seriously keep an eye on them as they burn easily!

To make your classic burger assemble by starting with a squirt of tomato sauce on your bun, then layer on your fillings in this order: 2 pieces of bacon, 2–3 slices of tomato, your meat patty with cheese already melted on top, fried egg, slice of beetroot, some grated carrot, slices of cucumber, some lettuce, followed by the top of the bun. Eat and, yes, it gets messy!

Makes 6–8 patties

It's hard to go past this stew on a cold winter's night and it is very delicious the next day for lunch—if you have any left over, that is. It's a pretty easy dish to make and an important one to teach the rug rats how to cook because it is all about the quality of the ingredients. Learning about the quality of ingredients teaches kids to respect our farmers and our produce.

EASY LAMB STEW

2 tablespoons olive oil

8 chump chops with bone in (about 200–250 g/ 7–9 oz each)

1 large onion, chopped

3 celery stalks, roughly chopped

2 large carrots, peeled and each cut into 8 chunks

2 parsnips, each cut into 6 chunks

3 potatoes, peeled and cut into quarters

1 teaspoon rosemary leaves (or dried if you don't have fresh)

500 ml (17 fl oz/2 cups) chicken stock

1 bouquet garni

salt and freshly ground black pepper

32 green beans, top and tailed

2 teaspoons cornflour (cornstarch)

2 tablespoons chopped flat-leaf (Italian) parsley

Heat 1 tablespoon of the olive oil in a large flameproof casserole dish over medium–high heat. Add the chops and brown on both sides. When done remove from the dish and set aside on a plate.

Put the remaining oil in the same dish, add the onion and fry for a couple of minutes—this is more to flavour the oil than to cook the onion. Next, add the celery, carrot, parsnip, potato and rosemary, fry for another couple of minutes, then return the chops to the dish along with any cooking juices. Add the stock and as much water as needed to cover the meat and vegetables—about 750 ml (26 fl oz/3 cups). Tuck the bouquet garni in under the meat, season with salt and pepper, bring to the boil, then reduce to a gentle simmer and cover with the lid. Cook for about 1½ hours, then add the green beans and cook for another 10 minutes. The meat should be very tender and the vegetables cooked through, but not cooked to mush.

Put the cornflour in a small bowl, add 1–2 tablespoons of cold water and mix until smooth. Add this to the stew and mix through—this will thicken the liquid and make it slightly viscous which is one of the reasons I love this simple stew. Lastly, taste for seasoning and adjust as needed—it will most likely require more salt, dig up the bouquet garni and discard.

Serve equally between four bowls and garnish with the parsley. Perfect cold night fare!

Feeds 4

I love it when I can start to feel the chill in the air. That means winter is just around the corner and with it comes along a whole lot of produce and recipes that I just love to cook. This recipe is certainly one of them. I always get excited when I see the first big, beautiful, deep red rhubarb stalks all bundled up together waiting to be bought and taken home and turned into a jam, coulis, chutney, added to soup, rabbit pie or a sour cake, and of course paired with its best friend, the apple, and put into a crumble!

APPLE AND RHUBARB CRUMBLE

4 granny smith apples, peeled, cored and cut into bite-sized pieces (to yield about 4 cups)

1 bunch rhubarb, washed and cut into 2 cm (¾ in) lengths (to yield about 4 cups)

raw sugar

grated zest of ½ lemon

45 g (1⅔ oz/½ cup) desiccated coconut

75 g (2⅔ oz/½ cup) plain (all-purpose) flour

50 g (1¾ oz/½ cup) rolled (porridge) oats

25 g (1 oz/¼ cup) flaked almonds

35 g (1¼ oz/¼ cup) crushed macadamia nuts

60 g (2¼ oz) butter, plus 1 tablespoon extra

2 tablespoons maple syrup

Preheat the oven to 200°C (400°F) (fan-forced 180°C/350°F).

Weigh the apple and the rhubarb so you can work out how much sugar to use. The rule of thumb I use is the amount of sugar to stew with the fruit is a quarter of the weight of the fruit. So if your fruit weighs 800 g (1 lb 12 oz) you would use 200 g (7 oz) of sugar. After you have worked this out put the apple and rhubarb pieces in a saucepan and then tip in the correct amount of sugar and the lemon zest. Put the pan on the stovetop over medium heat and give it all a good mix to coat the apple and rhubarb with the sugar. Cook, stirring occasionally, until the fruit is tender and has broken down. You still want to have chunks of fruit so don't cook it too long or else you will end up with a thick sludge—about 15 minutes should do it.

While the fruit is stewing get a large bowl and tip in the coconut, flour, rolled oats, almonds and macadamia nuts and give them all a good stir. Gently heat the butter and maple syrup together in a small saucepan over medium heat until melted, stirring to combine, then tip this into the combined dry ingredients. Mix thoroughly—this is your crumble topping.

Get a rectangular or oval-shaped ovenproof dish and use the extra butter to grease it. Tip in the stewed fruit and juices then cover with the crumble mixture.

Bake for about 25–30 minutes or until the crumble is a lovely golden brown. Serve the crumble with some ice cream or cream. Enjoy!

Feeds 4–6

Sometimes when things are easy to put together it feels like you are cheating—this recipe is a classic example of that. A tin of this and a tin of that, something or other out of a packet, maybe a healthy splash of milk from the carton, add a bit of heat and there you have it—cheat's lychee rice pudding. Deliciously sweet, filling, fragrant and above all simple.

CHEAT'S LYCHEE RICE PUDDING

220 g (7¾ oz/1 cup) arborio rice*
2 tins (270 ml/9½ fl oz each) coconut milk

2 tins (560 g/1 lb 4 oz each) lychees
   (juice reserved), cut into thirds
2 tablespoons brown sugar

Put the rice in a saucepan, add 500 ml (17 fl oz/2 cups) of the coconut milk and 500 ml (17 fl oz/2 cups) of the reserved lychee juice. Mix through the sugar and place the saucepan over medium–high heat, stir, bring to the boil then reduce the heat to a low simmer. Cook for about 30–35 minutes, covered, and stir often until the rice is cooked. If the mixture starts to look too dry, add in a little more lychee juice or even some milk from the fridge to keep it nice and moist.

Add the chopped lychees, stir through and turn off the heat. If you can stop yourself from eating it while it is still steaming hot good luck! I normally let it cool a little before tucking in. It will last in the fridge, covered, for a couple of days and it is easy to heat up in the microwave at 2 in the morning if the need arises.

Feeds 4–6

NOTE

Normally with risotto rice you want it to be *al dente* or have a little bit of bite to it, but for rice pudding you want to cook it past this point —not mushy but soft without the bite.

Acknowledgements

I am very happy to be writing the next couple of paragraphs as, in truth, without the support and help of a whole bunch of people I'm about to mention, you wouldn't be reading this! In fact, you wouldn't be holding this book or be able to sample the wonderful recipes inside—I can say that because I've cooked and eaten every recipe in this book several times and seriously think they are wonderful!

So to all the crew at Murdoch Books I say a very big heartfelt thank you. To the Publishing Director Sue Hines I say, 'Yay, we finally did it!!' I first met Sue in the late '90s when I pitched an idea I had about writing a cookbook using beer as an ingredient! I did eventually end up writing that book for Murdoch Books back in 2011. I am very grateful that Sue and I met up again a couple of years ago and gave me her full support to put this book together—many thanks to you.

Of course, Sue and I couldn't do it without the rest of the team involved and may I just say they are a talented and passionate bunch of people! To my Publisher at Murdoch Books, Corinne Roberts, thank you for your guidance, your patience and your support. To Emma Hutchinson, Project Manager extraordinaire thank you—you made it fun, you made it easy and you gave me energy when I was flagging! Oh, and you did a great job too! To Hugh Ford, Design Manager, and Justin Thomas, Designer, I say thank you from the bottom of my empty soup bowl, you guys did an awesome job on this book as always! Hopefully, we can do it all again sometime. Thanks to the shoot team—Brett Stevens for the fantastic photos, Rhianne Contrera for the beautiful styling of the food and Nick Banbury for cooking the dishes for the photos.

This is the third cook book I have written. Writing books is a labour of love and passion, and a lifestyle, so I would like to thank my beautiful, supportive and wonderful family for allowing me to indulge in this endeavour. I know it is not always easy as I know I do get a little bit obsessive about food, ingredients and shopping. So I say thank you for coming along on the journey. To my wife, Andrea, thank you for eating the dishes I cooked and giving me your honest feedback even if I didn't like to hear it. To my eldest daughter, Elise, and my youngest, Erin, thank you for cooking some of the dishes (several times over) until we got them right. To my middle daughter, Emily, it was ever so lovely to listen to you singing while I was cooking in the kitchen—thank you.

I would also like to thank my friends and followers on the various social media sites such as Twitter, Facebook, Instagram and the rest for giving me their support and feedback about the various dishes I posted. A big thank you also to the regulars at the Mornington Peninsula Brewery who, more often than not, where my impromptu taste testers on whatever I had cooked that day.

I loved writing this book and I hope that will you love it too! Now it's time to get your apron on, sharpen your knives, open the book to the first recipe and GET YOUR MOJO ON!

Index

Published in 2015 by Murdoch Books,
an imprint of Allen & Unwin

Murdoch Books Australia
83 Alexander Street
Crows Nest NSW 2065
Phone: +61 (0)2 8425 0100
Fax: +61 (0)2 9906 2218
murdochbooks.com.au
info@murdochbooks.com.au

Murdoch Books UK
Erico House, 6th Floor
93–99 Upper Richmond Road
Putney, London SW15 2TG
Phone: +44 (0) 20 8785 5995
murdochbooks.co.uk
info@murdochbooks.co.uk

For Corporate Orders & Custom Publishing
contact Noel Hammond,
National Business Development Manager,
Murdoch Books Australia

Publisher: Corinne Roberts
Design Manager: Hugh Ford
Designer: Justin Thomas
Editor: Emma Hutchinson
Photographer: Brett Stevens
Stylist: Rhianne Contrera
Production Manager: Mary Bjelobrk

A cataloguing-in-publication entry is available
from the catalogue of the National Library of
Australia at nla.gov.au.

ISBN 978 1 74196 897 2 Australia
ISBN 978 1 74336 181 8 UK

A catalogue record for this book is available
from the British Library.

Colour reproduction by Splitting Image
Colour Studio Pty Ltd, Clayton, Victoria
Printed by 1010 Printing International
Limited, China